Le Corbusier

Paris —————— **Chandigarh**

Klaus-Peter Gast

Le Corbusier
Paris ———— Chandigarh

**With a Foreword
by Arthur Rüegg**

Birkhäuser–Publishers for Architecture
Basel · Berlin · Boston

The following illustrations are reproduced by kind permission
of the Fondation Le Corbusier and of ProLitteris. For each of these
illustrations Copyright ProLitteris, 2000, 8033 Zürich and
© FLC – Paris, 2000:
Pages 15, 18, 19, 24, 25 middle and bottom, 26, 27 left, 34, 35 top
and bottom, 39, 40 left, 41 left and right, 57 bottom, 81, 82 top and
bottom, 83 top and bottom, 84 top and bottom, 95 bottom, 99,
102, 105 left and right, 123 top and bottom, 130 bottom, 147
bottom, 163, 172, 178, 179, 180 top and bottom, 181, 182, 183,
184, 185 left and right, 187

All other photographs and drawings are by the author.

Translation from German: Michael Robinson

Design and Production: Atelier Fischer, Berlin
Typesetting and Lithography: LVD GmbH, Berlin
Printing: Messedruck Leipzig GmbH
Binding: Kunst- und Verlagsbuchbinderei, Leipzig

This book is also available in a German language edition (ISBN
3–7643–6088–7)

A CIP catalogue record for this book is available from the Library of
Congress, Washington D. C., USA

Deutsche Bibliothek Cataloging-in-Publication Data

Gast, Klaus-Peter:
Le Corbusier, Paris - Chandigarh / Klaus-Peter Gast. With a
foreword by Arthur Rüegg. [Transl. from German: Michael
Robinson]. - Basel ; Berlin ; Boston : Birkhäuser, 2000
    Dt. Ausg. u.d.T.: Gast, Klaus-Peter: Le Corbusier,
    Paris - Chandigarh
    ISBN 3-7643-6291-X

© 2000 Birkhäuser – Publishers for Architecture, P. O.Box 133,
CH-4010 Basel, Switzerland

© 2000 Fondation Le Corbusier
for the works of Le Corbusier

Printed on acid-free paper produced from chlorine-free pulp. TFC ∞
Printed in Germany
ISBN 3–7643–6291-X

9 8 7 6 5 4 3 2 1

Contents

Foreword
by Arthur Rüegg

Even the "primitive" master builders – said Le Corbusier in the magazine *L'Esprit Nouveau*[1] in 1921 – had defined modules with potentials for repetitive use, and applied elementary geometrical rules to simplify their search for solutions to their building tasks. But the Greek and Egyptian masters, then Michelangelo and Blondel after them, he goes on to say, used so-called "tracés régulateurs" (literally: regulating lines) firstly to perfect their designs and secondly to satisfy a spirit striving for artistic and mathematical perfection. Le Corbusier's argument leaves us in no doubt that great architecture is geometrically regular. He points out that there was no break in this tradition until the 20th century: *"The man of to-day employs nothing at all and the result is the* boulevard Raspail. *But he proclaims that he is a free poet and that his instincts suffice …"*
Passages like this must have been explosive, written as they are by a notoriously progressive architect who had thrown the empty shells of all historical styles overboard. As the inventor of the concept of the "machine à habiter", he would seem at first glance to be one of these functionalists averse to any formalist argument. But it is not possible to get to the heart of Le Corbusier in any simple way. Indeed, at the same time he defined architecture as *"the skilful, accurate and magnificent play of masses seen in light"*, thus concentrating exclusively on the observer's experience conveyed in forms. Apparent contradictions like this have always been disturbing. Bruno Taut, for example, was relating above all to the "artistic" aspect of Le Corbusier's work when he wrote in 1929: "His architecture will never upset the middle-class world. It is based on a highly talented aesthetic of the *salons*. Here the architect is building as a painter in his studio paints his pictures, i.e. he is building pictures."[2]
It is a particular quality of Le Corbusier's buildings that they can be read in different ways. And so a crucial aspect of his design approach lies in the possibility of placing opposite poles in a state of tension and in doing so synthesizing them in one and the same building. So Le Corbusier the functionalist had no trouble in taking on a fight with the *Ecole des Beaux-Arts*, which represented the continuity of a building culture based on historical values – while at the same time as an "artist" he was propagating the composition of his own purified forms with the aid of geometrical formal laws –

just as architects like Michelangelo or Blondel had so perfectly demonstrated.
Unlike Louis Kahn (to whom Klaus-Peter Gast devoted a first analysis two years ago) Le Corbusier himself was not trained at the *Ecole des Beaux-Arts* in Paris, nor at a related institution. Since his early childhood he was influenced by the idea of composition in the spirit of geometrical and sculptural principles. Some years ago now, Marc Solitaire showed that Charles-Edouard Jeanneret (his real name) was crucially influenced by attending a local Froebel school from the age of just under four.[3] Another indication can be found in material for teaching drawing at "Ecoles primaires" – a few sheets are shown here –, which appeared in La Chaux-de-Fonds in 1894 – the very year that Charles-Edouard started at primary school himself. It seems that the children were even taught to understand and construct plant forms with the aid of geometrical constructions. From then on it was only a small step to Charles L'Eplattenier's exercises. L'Eplattenier was the key teacher at the local art school, in which geometrical versions of natural forms were combined to form ornaments. Jeanneret, as a self-educated person, later acquired a great deal of further knowledge about the secrets of architectural composition on his travels and in the great libraries of France and Germany, and not least during his practical training periods under the Perret brothers in Paris and Peter Behrens in Berlin. Thus the geometrical elements that Klaus-Peter Gast has identified in Charles-Edouard Jeanneret's early buildings designed for La Chaux-de-Fonds seem to be a perfectly natural component of a design approach that is ultimately shaped by classicism. The seamless continuation of this practice during the period of "abstract", purist architecture is astonishing at first glance, but readily comprehensible, as the kind of matter he was dealing with here was devising proportions for and arranging windows in a rectangular façade – in other words a purely artistic problem.
Le Corbusier – as he called himself from 1920 – reflected about working with the "tracés régulateurs" in various essays at that time.[4] He made a distinction between the "tracé automatique", which is produced to a certain extent automatically by constructive propositions – for example by the arrangement of "pilotis" (columns) that remain visible, always equally spaced. In this way a regular cadence of building parts of the same kind are produced. In the different case of the "tracé numérique" the cadence follows a simple whole-number progression – for example in the sequence of bands of windows and parapets of different widths. Finally different areas relate harmoniously on the basis of

9

[1] Le Corbusier, "Les tracés régulateurs", in: L'Esprit Nouveau no. 5, pp. 563–572; the article was reprinted in: Le Corbusier, "Vers une architecture", Paris 1923, pp. 49–63; English edition: Towards a New Architecture", London 1927/99, p. 65–83.
[2] Bruno Taut, "Krisis der Architektur", in: Wohnungswirtschaft issue 8, vol. 6/1929.
[3] Marc Solitaire, "Le Corbusier et l'urbain: la rectification du damier froebelien", in: La ville et l'urbanisme après Le Corbusier, actes d'un colloque, La Chaux-de-Fonds 1993, pp. 93–117, and recently in the (unpublished) dissertation "Le Corbusier – le don de Jeanneret et les dons de Froebel", ETH Zurich 1998.
[4] Cf. note 1 and: Le Corbusier, "Architecture d'époque machiniste", in: Journal de psychologie normale et pathologique, XXIII, 1926. The quotations used here come from: Le Corbusier, "Tracés régulateurs", in: L'architecture vivante, printemps et été 1929, pp. 13–23. Cf. on this subject: D. M. (Dario Matteoni), "Tracés régulateurs", in: Le Corbusier. Une encyclopédie, Paris 1987, pp. 409–424.

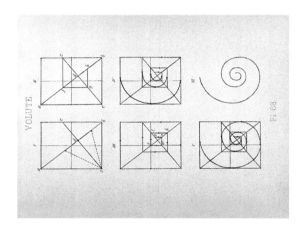

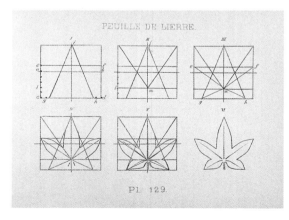

„Cours de Dessin pour Ecoles primaires,"
Lithographies by A. Chateau, La Chaux-de-Fonds 1894

their proportional similarity; in the "tracé sur diagonale" the proportions are controlled with the aid of the diagonals of areas.

Sometimes it was necessary to use several kinds of "tracés" that overlap. Le Corbusier himself provides us with the complicated set of rules for the Villa Stein/de Monzie and the Pavillon Church, but also with the set of rules for the Mundaneum project in Geneva. But he warns about abuse in the same breath: he says that when using these tracés one is not dealing with absolute formulae that can simply be carried over to something else; they must be subjected to careful artistic judgement in every new case. (Even in 1921 he was fulminating about merely being in love with planning graphics, something he identified above all in the circle around the *Ecole des Beaux-Arts* in Paris; in his view this simply leads to an "illusion des plans".) He says that the "tracé régulateur" used as he felt it should be is merely a method that can "give a three-dimensional composition – a building, an image or a sculpture – a very great element of precision as far as its proportions are concerned". He adds that it is impossible to give a building poetic qualities by using "tracés", but the intention behind the design can be clarified and confirmed.

The "tracés régulateurs" are first and foremost a design aid, but they can also be used for analysis and thus serve man's old urge to find the key to the secret of perfectly proportioned works. Le Corbusier knew and commented on the works of Matila Ghyka,[5] which present attempts that have been rampant since the mid 19th century to interpret grand architecture of the past on the basis of mathematical and geometrical laws. Le Corbusier himself sought to legitimize his approach by identifying historical models: for example by analysing the Capitol in Rome, the Grand Trianon in Versailles or the Porte Saint-Denis in Paris. Incidentally Lucien Schwob, an old painter friend from La Chaux-de-Fonds, dedicated his book *Réalité de l'Art*,[6] which appeared in 1954, largely to the geometrical analysis of famous pictures, including Pablo Picasso's "Guernica". And so this allows us to point out that the "tracés" were used not least by painters, and this includes the Purists Amédée Ozenfant and Charles-Edouard Jeanneret.

Alongside the location of the right angle and the square it is above all the Golden Section that determines Le Corbusier's tracés. Even in 1920 the Golden Section was part of the programme of *L'Esprit Nouveau*, as an example of an invariable formal rule in art that it was even possible to prove by means of improvised tests on randomly chosen individuals.[7] In the early forties Le Corbusier took up his analysis of the Golden Section again with the Modulor (published 1950). The starting

[5] Matila Ghyka, "Esthétique des proportions dans la nature et dans les arts", Paris 1927, and: Matila Ghyka, "Le Nombre d'or", Paris 1931.
[6] Lucien Schwob, "Réalité de l'Art", Lausanne 1954.
[7] Cf. "Note de la rédaction", in: L'Esprit Nouveau no. 1, 1920.

point for the two series of numbers in the Modulor are certain dimensions of the human figure and an anthropometry that sees the Golden Section as a constant ratio of the different parts of the human body to each other. With the Modulor, Le Corbusier succeeded in defining a common, harmoniously proportioned system of measurements for man and for the framework of his life (architecture).

Klaus-Peter Gast does not analyse Le Corbusier's work on the basis of the master's own theories, but uses a method developed from historical buildings in a different context. In contrast with the widespread interest in the lines controlling façades, he concentrates on the composition of the ground plans. It is not surprising that the results of his investigations confirm Le Corbusier's use of the square and the Golden Section. What is much more exciting is the fact that even long after the Purist phase Le Corbusier was still working on the basis of geometrical constructions. It seems that the Modulor and the "tracé régulateur" are by no means mutually exclusive. What at first determined the rhythm of the Purist volumes and their surface composition finally became a device for disciplining additive structures. The design for a large hospital complex in Venice (not presented here) is a most vivid demonstration of this development.

Klaus-Peter Gast's analyses provide insights into the horizontal dimension of a series of buildings through all phases of the architect's work. He thus develops highly stimulating interpretations of individual designs, but also gives us a new view of change and constancy within certain design parameters in Le Corbusier's work.

Introduction

Le Corbusier's[1] work includes some of the 20th century's most important and influential architecture. His was one of the great pioneering achievements in the development of Modern architecture in its classical phase, but he also pointed the way forwards for other architectural movements from the forties onwards: Brutalism, for example, or the new type of Expressionism that emerged after the fifties. There was a flood of publications after his work became famous in the twenties, and especially after his death in 1965, and we have to justify adding another analysis of Le Corbusier to those that already exist.

The present book does not follow the trend of throwing together collections of material and presenting them as a "new and up-to-date documentation", and it is definitely not a contribution to the "archaeology of the psyche" of an architect that is so beloved of historians in particular, where the whole point is to pursue psychological factors that could have helped to shape his work. Such diligent ferreting for possible models, stimuli and and phenomena is not the main concern here. The present work attempts to get closer to Le Corbusier by applying concrete analysis to the rational aspect of design, something that quite clearly shaped the construction of Le Corbusier's architecture. Rationality as a comprehensible principle is to be found mainly in the *geometrical structure* of a given design, and the complexity of that structure needs to be deciphered and interpreted. Here the question of inherent *order* arises, governing the individual design but also the work as a whole. A key component of the following analysis will be to show how order is expressed in the work of Le Corbusier, and the geometrical *figures* that pervade that order (see fig. 1).

According to Brook's most recent monumental portrayal of Le Corbusier's early "formative years",[2] the architect's perception of geometry and proportion as important overall aspects of design began to emerge in the period around 1910. He mentions influences during Le Corbusier's stay in Germany, above all by August Thiersch, possibly Theodor Fischer and definitely Peter Behrens, for whom Le Corbusier worked, still as Charles-Edouard Jeanneret, for a few months in 1911. But even in his early years, in other words still in the 19th century, geometry has certainly played a significant role as a design principle in his training and work as a clock engraver. At this time design awareness, under the powerful influence of the Ecole des Beaux-Arts in Paris, tended towards structures based on symmetries, axes and proportions. Jeanneret was a great admirer of the way in which natural structures were put together, for example the Jura fir, which was ubiquitous as a design motif. On the basis of this, and of his teacher Charles L'Eplattenier's crucial suggestions, he built up an awareness of order to a quite unusual degree of sensitivity. Jeanneret still disapproved of the Italian Renaissance in 1907, but he admired Charles Rennie Mackintosh's work shown at an exhibition in Vienna in the same year. 1908 saw his first decisive stay in Paris, when he worked with Auguste Perret, a new father figure and the important person who showed him how reinforced concrete could be used in a clear structural composition. Jeanneret was still at odds with himself as a character in 1911, and he allowed himself to be influenced by a whole variety of trends that he came across. Then on his important *voyage d'Orient* he discovered the great works of classical architecture, the Parthenon in Athens, Rome with Michelangelo and Hadrian's Villa and the Piazza dei Miracoli in Pisa. Here ancient, timeless geometrical manifestations were enthusiastically praised and profoundly internalized. Le Corbusier's views changed after the painter Amédée Ozenfant had introduced him to Cubism, which was such an important movement in the art world, and then led to the Purism that shaped both Ozenfant and Jeanneret. The picture "La Cheminée", which Jeanneret painted at this time, stood both as a profession of faith and a farewell to his earlier phase of development. From 1920 onwards, simple geometrical figurations were conceived on canvas with meticulous precision, but also in a new way that combined overlapping and *transparency*. They formed the substantial basis for the great creative phase that was about to begin.

Fig. 1

The geometrical figures inherent in Le Corbusier's designs, predominantly in the form of square, circle or rectangle with defined proportions, can usually not be discerned directly, but are always present. Once they are revealed, connections, links and logical sequences can be seen that lead to fundamental aspects of the designer's thinking. At the same time this brings out the irrational component by creating contrast, and it is legitimate to ask how this contrasting pair, rationality and irrationality, appear in Le Corbusier, how they relate, and what the quality of this relation is. At first the irrational element is always a component of the start of the design in the form of an intuitive *idea*, which is subjective in character because of the architect's world of experience and insight. But in the course of our argument it becomes clear that Le Corbusier deliberately includes irrational components as the genesis of the design pro-

[1] Le Corbusier's cousin Pierre Jeanneret was closely associated with the name Le Corbusier from the designs for the Citrohan House onwards. He played a considerable role in the buildings and designs produced between 1922 and 1940, and later with the Chandigarh designs, sacrificing himself for the sake of this city's development. Many buildings not mentioned here were built independently by Pierre Jeanneret in Chandigarh.

[2] H. Allen Brooks, "Le Corbusier's Formative Years", Chicago, London 1997. For this see also: Paul Venable Turner, "The Education of Le Corbusier. A Study of the Development of Le Corbusier's Thought 1900–1920", Harvard thesis1971, New York 1977; Mary Patricia May Sekler: "The Early Drawings of Charles-Edouard Jeanneret (Le Corbusier) 1902–1908", Harvard thesis 1973, New York 1977.

ceeds. They are auratic in character and expand the dimensions of a particular design by adding a plane that is more difficult to understand, but still open to perception.

Deciphering the rational principles starts with the documents produced by Le Corbusier, in other words his plan drawings. This is where the research starts, as the plan, as a – usually authentic – image of what is to be built allows the most precise statements possible to be made. Precise drawing counts as a precise image of the design, and therefore is an ideal way of approaching the idea that is "frozen" within the plan. The system of interdependent geometrical figurations can best be presented analytically from the working plan, i. e. the last one to be made, and the closest to the building. Sketches can illustrate and explain how the design emerges from the irrational, intuitive side, and show a subjective approach to the finding of ideas. But the concrete design image furnished by the working plan, translated into clearly delimited lines, means decision, consolidation, calculation and the translation of ideas into form.

The method used here is *plan analysis*, which was developed by Harmen Thies[3] and applied by the author[4] to other 20th century examples. It aims to show the emergence of each design step by step, i. e. to discover the interdependent, rationally comprehensible stages of development through which it goes, and which are preserved in the final plan, and to put them into the form of a logical *system*. The build-up of the design can then be seen as a sequence of individual geometrical figures and is deciphered as *a system of figurative geometry*.

Precise architectural analysis can only happen if suppositions and assumptions that are present at the outset are supported by unambiguous statements. The sources of information available here in the form of descriptions frequently turn out to be individually interpreted: in other words they are alienating presentations with restrictive viewpoints. In contrast with this, concrete comprehensibility and logical derivation will be central to the following observations. Thus a proven result will emerge as part of a logical process. It is our intention that not the observer, in other words the interpreter, of the work will speak, but the work itself.

When using the rational method chosen here the start of the design has to be clearly defined: a starting point or better a *starting figure* has to be determined. This is the only point of departure that can be rationally valid as a hypothetical start for the design, and it is only from this that a sequence can be generated. It is from the starting figure, for example the square or the circle, that geometrical and proportional figures are derived successively by defining the edges and the way in which they relate within a plan structure. These edges emerge from the traces of the walls in the ground plans, which start to relate to each other in the process. In their turn, the edges define the borders of areas, and thus the areas that define the ground plan can unfold as geometrical figures within a hierarchy.

The focal point of the second half of the book is an examination of the Capitol complex in Chandigarh. Here geometrical order is not just at the core of the designs for the individual buildings, but it is also in the foreground of the overall composition of the ensemble. The main point of this section was to examine the *disposition* of the parts, to fathom the way in which they fit together and depend on each other. Here plan analysis provides new and surprising insights that fit compellingly into Le Corbusier's intellectual world of geometry and proportion, particularly at that time. Today, 50 years after the birth of this difficult Chandigarh enterprise, a new critical appraisal with a different emphasis seems appropriate and necessary.

The present book examines selected buildings and projects in chronological order, from both the important early phase of the œuvre and the late work. The key here is not a comprehensive or even complete presentation of the work as a whole, but a specific approach that proves a suspected continuity within the work. The analysis begins with the Villa Schwob, an important transitional building dating from 1916, and shows that Le Corbusier started to use the rational design principles described here at an early stage. Important buildings in the twenties were followed by the transitional wartime period when Le Corbusier broadened his theoretical grasp of urban development and proportion. These principles were then put into practice in the post-war period and led to new aesthetic categories – but Le Corbusier still continued to apply principles of order intensively. As well as a drawing-based analysis of scaled geometrical figures, the present observations at the same time provide a new critical description of the buildings and projects. Here aspects of these examples that have so far not received much consideration come to the fore. Plan analysis does emphasize the rationally comprehensible principle of the designs, but the world of geometrically evident rationality frequently occurs as a point of intersection between aspects of the designs that are clearly comprehensible *and* merely perceptible, indeed almost metaphysical.

Le Corbusier's early work consists of cubic, mainly white structures. But in fact a new aesthetic does assert itself after his designs for the villas De Mandrot near Marseilles (1929–32) and Errazuris in Chile (1930), the weekend house near Paris and the Aux Mathes house by the sea (both 1935). This is clearly different from the language that had become a dogma through self-im-

---

[3] First use of plan analysis in Harmen H. Thies, "Grundrißfiguren Balthasar Neumanns: Zum maßstäblich geometrischen Rißaufbau der Schönbornkapelle und der Hofkirche in Würzburg", Florence 1980; and Harmen H. Thies, "Michelangelo. Das Kapitol", published by the Florence Institute of Art History, Munich 1982.

[4] Klaus-Peter Gast, "Louis I. Kahn. The Idea of Order", Basel, Berlin, Boston 1998.

posed rules, which was later known as Modern architecture or, in German, "klassische Moderne". As shown in the first part of this book, Le Corbusier did not necessarily keep to these rules even for his own buildings; in fact it is much easier to see that they tend towards a "theory" that needed to be freshly formulated. With the emergence of Fascism in Europe and the subsequent Second World War, Le Corbusier's activities broke off, even though he was already world-famous by the late twenties. His theoretical work, relating to an architectural language open to clear articulation, also paled. Certainly his intensive work on urban planning questions, which started at this time, should also be taken into consideration. This took him away from fixed dogmas, but despite all this a different spirit starts to show in the mid-thirties designs. Finding the reason for this "break" is not the object of the present work. Much more interesting is the question of the extent to which a *continuity* of principles can be identified that makes the œuvre as a whole seem like a uniform structure. It seems obvious that there is no actual break, but that certain aesthetic categories simply shift and – this is presented in detail for the first time in this publication – a clearly recognizable principle of continuity is present.

The case in point is the complex subject of geometrical order, which – and this is the crucial point – determines the structure of all Le Corbusier's designs. This order is almost independent of considerations of "form" in terms of standards, dogmas or categories, and turns out to be applicable with a high degree of flexibility. It combines geometry and proportion within a system that is inherent to the designs. Le Corbusier has himself described in detail that he always used geometry and proportion as principles of a comprehensive order. As can be seen from the following examples, this order appears in the creative process as an expression of a universal language and as such contributes strongly to the designs' timeless character.

Fig. 1 Charles-Edouard Jeanneret (Le Corbusier): „La Cheminée, 1918"

Villa Schwob
1916 La Chaux-de-Fonds Switzerland

The Villa Schwob is often rightly defined as a work that concludes an early phase in Le Corbusier's work; he was still known as Charles-Edouard Jeanneret at the time. This private house was the last of a series of six Le Corbusier was able to build in his home town at a very early age – the experienced local architect René Chapallaz helped him with the first five. But the Villa Schwob is already a transitional element within his career, which was already starting to look as though it would be unusual: this villa does not fit in at all with the previous buildings, which form a group in their own right. The Fallet, Stotzer, Jaquemet, Jeanneret-Perret and Favre-Jacot houses (built in that order from 1906 to 1914)[5] still follow a fundamentally classical building canon. Admittedly they display, following Le Corbusier's personal development, stylistic variations ranging from romantic and regional proto-Art Nouveau to stocky classicism. But here the question is not where the form of a building component, stylistic element of or quotation from the architect's store of memories came from, just as no detailed journey back to the roots is intended in the following parallels between the Villa Schwob and some earlier buildings.

Anatole Schwob, who commissioned the house, had earned a fortune by making watches in La Chaux-de-Fonds, which was the world precision chronometer centre at that time. He commissioned the 29-year-old Le Corbusier (Jeanneret) to build a villa after the young man had been recommended by his cousin Raphy Schwob, who had seen his earlier houses. Le Corbusier produced a ground plan that followed the concept of a design from Auguste Perret's office in Paris, in which he had worked for a time. Schwob himself is said to have chosen this concept for the so-called "maison bouteille" – it was shaped like a stubby bottle with the roof blending fluently into the outer walls – as an idea for his own house from the architect's portfolio of designs.[6]

Fig. 2
The original design proposes a square outline for the plan, with semicircular protrusions like large apses thrusting out on two opposite sides. A centrally-placed two-storey hall is proposed in the entirely symmetrical outline of this first suggestion, opening on to the garden. This basic scheme was retained until the final design, but with one crucial change: an entrance foyer with staircase building is added on the street side and a second, set-back storey placed on top as a kind of penthouse. Schwob himself changed Le Corbusier's pro-

posal by asking that the volume should be doubled in this way. Interestingly enough, Le Corbusier did not develop a new concept despite such a major amendment. He kept to the initial design – square with protrusions at the side – and simply added the requested extensions, plonking Schwob's additional volume on top of his own, which seems to have a plan figure that cannot be shifted or changed. Thus the process of changing the initial design is documented and declared to be part of the final design.

The impression is of a centred figure that also has markedly axial orientation. As well as this, two single-storey wings are added beside the staircase section, containing side rooms on the left-hand side and a roofed terrace on the right. If the ground plans of earlier designs are compared, for example the ground floors of the Stotzer and Jaquement houses, then it becomes clear that the form of a directional body with side protrusions is built into these ground plans as well. These buildings were designed in parallel during Le Corbusier's stay in Vienna in 1907. However different they may appear in view, their ground plan concepts show that they are buildings of the same type. The two houses are on adjacent building plots on a slope with a sweeping view of the Jura landscape. They are oriented with their main rooms facing the view and with access from the rear. This makes them *directional* volumes, showing up as rectangular buildings with side ratios of almost identical dimensions. It is significant that the openings in the longitudinal walls are concentrated in a zone that is clearly defined on both sides and confined essentially to the rear section. They are supported by pier-like extremities thrusting into the exterior space, and clearly tend in a counter-direction, in other words they constitute a *counter-movement*. The piers are opposite each other on the two sides, and define a kind of latent, rectangular layer of space that is interrupted by the steps and the dividing walls but is such a striking presence that it seems to be quite unambiguously intentional. In contrast with this, parts of the longitudinal walls are completely closed. This motif will become important in later work.

The design for the Jaquemet House corresponds exactly in terms of dimensions and the basic form of the building, the positioning of the access area and the steps, the distribution of the interior functions, down to the wall pier outlines and window divisions (see fig. 4), but the counter-movement of two directions and the overlapping of two spatial outlines is increased further. The longitudinal walls thrust far out in the garden area and on the entrance side to form an external boundary, to the point of stretching the plan figure. The extended garden steps also add to this impression. In

Fig. 3
Fig. 4

[5] For this see detailed studies by Brooks and Turner: Brooks, "Le Corbusier's Formative Years", and Turner, "The Education of Le Corbusier. A Study of the Development of Le Corbusier's Thought 1900–1920".
[6] For this see William J. Curtis, "Le Corbusier. Ideas and Forms", London 1986, p. 44.

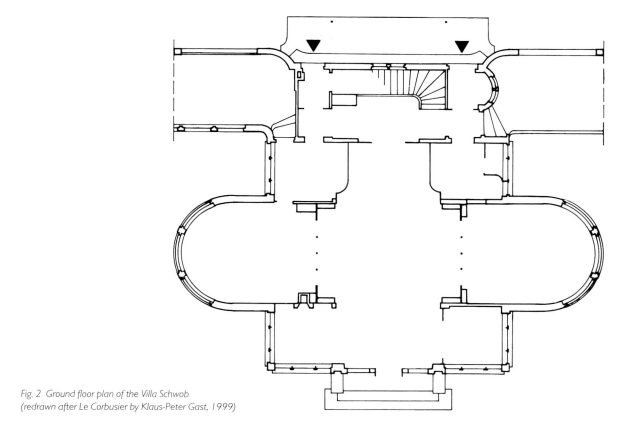

Fig. 2 Ground floor plan of the Villa Schwob
(redrawn after Le Corbusier by Klaus-Peter Gast, 1999)

Fig. 3 Ground floor of the Villa Stotzer
(redrawn after Le Corbusier by Klaus-Peter Gast, 1999)

Fig. 4 Ground floor of the Villa Jaquemet
(redrawn after Le Corbusier by Klaus-Peter Gast, 1999)

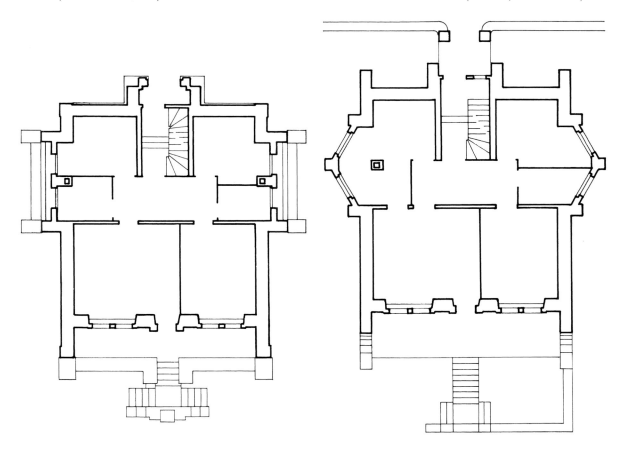

contrast with this, the "apses", i.e. the concentrated opening areas with their windows thrusting diagonally outwards and a wall pier in the middle of each try to reinforce the counter-movement. Their positioning on the diagonal is the *first evident attempt in Le Corbusier's architecture* to translate a suggestion of movement directly into physical forms.

This process of movement also becomes visible in the Villa Schwob ground plan (see fig. 2). The staircase built on in the middle of the back gives the originally rigid, non-directional figure of the square a direction that is additionally confirmed by the central, two-storey hall living-room with two-storey glazing facing the garden. The rooms placed here in the middle of the "longitudinal walls" of the square are also expanded to the sides in the form of dramatic curves. This all makes it clear that the lateral outward movement in this design means considerably more than in the case of the Villa Jaquemet. In fact it produces a transverse, obviously coherent transparent area divided off only by glazed doors. This overlaps with the hall living-room that is arranged at right angles to it, producing a *doubly assigned* central zone. This concentricity of the main room is so important to Le Corbusier that he only proposes skylight windows in all the corners of the square, which form rooms in their own right because of this arrangement, so that it is absolutely clear in the façade as well that they are "side rooms" with no outlook. Remembering the earlier houses, the "longitudinal walls" therefore remain mostly closed, so that one can assume that this is a further development of this original thought. But the outward-thrusting, curved rooms are opened up with large areas of French windows, giving the impression of a wall thinned and tensioned by dynamic extension, until only narrow columns remain within the plane of the wall. This dynamic quality, created by precisely calculated curves, contrasts with the rigidity of the square figure. In the Villa Schwob we see the first signs of the struggle that is later so intense in Le Corbusier's work between a rationally developed orthogonal figure and a figuration invented with passionate intuition and later often completely free. There are other curved wall figures appearing in this ground plan for the first time that also point in this direction: the narrow walls in the hall entrance area, the curved wall in the bathroom and the outward curving wall in the main entrance area. This forms a convex-concave figure in combination with the curves in the side wings running along the street. Their curves, nestling symmetrically up to the staircase section to indicate the two entrances are reminiscent of the access wall of the Villa Jaquement (see fig. 4), which also takes this form, and leans gently against the entrance roof piers. The side room and terrace wing of

View from the garden

the Villa Schwob can be read formally as a transformation of the Villa Jaquemet's garden wall, especially as Le Corbusier is still very concerned at this time with the idea of making a connection with the topography or the immediate surroundings by using building sections that thrust a long way outwards — a function that was performed earlier by walls that ran out and were firmly anchored in the ground.

The design of the Villa Schwob represents an important step towards defining an independent architectural language for Le Corbusier. Here, by using new building technology and reinforced concrete, which he had learned to handle under Auguste Perret in Paris, Le Corbusier is entering the world of abstract formal thinking. The house type now emerges as a self-related, almost autonomous formal structure, dominated by a geometrical proposition. The step into abstraction was not an easy one for Jeanneret at the time, who was still committed to local convention. The hybrid character of the building can be explained in part by his being enlightened by numerous previous journeys. And Peter Behrens, in whose Berlin office Le Corbusier had worked previously, certainly prepared the way for abstract, geometrical thinking for him, as he had already done at about the same time for Walter Gropius and Ludwig Mies van der Rohe.[7] For Le Corbusier, going back to fundamental, almost archaic basic figures to produce reduced, prismatic bodies as almost undecorated, "pure" forms was a world of experience with new dimensions. The Villa Schwob also shows that this new world was not completely assimilated at first. Clamping the extended volume together with the building as originally designed was not without its problems at the points of overlap. It led to a strangely cramped collision between different volumes, exacerbated by a wall on both sides that was probably seen as a link between the staircase and the living-room section of the building. As well as this, the architect thought it necessary to decorate the horizontal concluding line of a flat-roofed building, which he was realizing for the first time here, with a greatly protruding, stepped cornice as a trough for plants, thus blurring the precision of this line and the geometrical figure that he had created. From this point on, geometry is increasingly a new leitmotif in his designs. In terms of weight it replaces nature, whose motifs had shaped his work until then – though again in abstract form. The rapturous and romantic element retires in favour of reasoned, rational thought. But rationality and emotion as poles remain a consistent component of his future output.

But the block-like simplification of the building with carefully calculated curves and newly emerging rationality does not refer to the new reinforced concrete skeleton building method. Le Corbusier had previously worked in Auguste Perret's Paris office. Perret was the pioneer of reinforced concrete building in France. His apartment house in rue Franklin concentrated the load on piers and thus made it possible to arrange the dividing walls relatively freely. Incidentally the set-back attic storey of the Villa Schwob could go back to Perret's

roof garden, which Le Corbusier admired. The construction method of the Villa Schwob, however, could only be seen clearly during the building phase; it is concealed inside the completed building. Only some lines of the columns in the central interior area are vaguely reminiscent of a grid construction principle with a load-bearing function and fundamentally allowing free plan design. Le Corbusier is *separating load-bearing function and envelope* for the first time here, but this is not shown or celebrated, but disappears in the lines of the interior dividing walls and the exterior walls.

Rigorous symmetry, flat roof, reduced ornament and the "naked" quality of the wall add up to "statements" of an architectural aesthetic that is developing in a new way. The homogeneous quality of the smooth brick wall, with its choice finish – forming an integrated whole – in fact places sculpture, i.e. self-illustrating form, in the foreground, rather than the house as a functional structure. The three-dimensional elemental geometry of the cube and of the cylinder that dissolves into the wall are part of a passionate composition for the first time in Le Corbusier's œuvre. "Self-"confident and close to time-lessness in its formal language, the building gives the impression of a kind of neutrality. The ground plan is also anything but a functionally developed formal

19

The building's position on a slope

⁷ For this see particularly Brooks, "Le Corbusier's Formative Years".

structure: it is a preconceived proposition into which functions can be scattered almost at random.

The role played by the newly discovered world of geometry, its crucial involvement in the development of the ground plan and the way in which it determined its emergence, will be demonstrated in the following analytical sequence. Calculated form as the result of primarily intuitive input comes into being in a *process* that can be shown in individual, interdependent steps. This is intended to make it clear that the dimensions of the parts of the building, the scale of lengths and areas in plan and elevation, the relationship between sets of lines inside and outside and their three-dimensional relations in space, in other words their *proportions*, all have a decisive part to play. These aspects appear even in this design and thus reveal Le Corbusier's awareness of their importance.

20

The starting point of the design is a square of a defined size. It is the idea and beginning of a developing concrete form that acquires increasing complexity. The square is both proposition and "form", in other words an autonomous figure, not a shape determined functionally by external requirements. Its four corners remain recognizable to the end of the development process and are later discernible in the building, and thus unambiguous. The square is not "deformed". **Fig. 5**

The square is divided up within its outer lines. Here column dimensions and a central area that is also square play a crucial role. Four columns of fixed dimensions are placed within the corners of the square, and they form a new trace along their inner edges. The middle of the enclosing square is now determined on two axes and a central square area defined. Two zones emerge: the central square zone and the zone extending to the traces of the corner columns. The central square area and the "extension area" at the side reaching to the inner traces of the corner columns thus together form the proportional area of the *Golden Section*.[8] In terms of geometry: the diagonal of half the central square zone describes an arc to the trace of the corner columns and determines the Golden Section area proportion through the intersection point with the "bottom line" of the diagonal. Columns of the same dimensions are now placed on the outside of the corners of the central square. Square corner zones are created by extending the sides of the centre square to the lines of the enclosing square. **Fig. 6**

The original square is thus divided up following a simple geometrical and proportional approach, in order to define the support points for the reinforced concrete skeleton.

The initial square now acquires columns of the same dimensions at all proportionally defined positions. Their inner and outer traces divide the overall area into three different zones: one is the central square zone, then the rectangular zones on each side, finally the ensuing corner zone with four squares. These zones form the structure of the supporting system of a rigid, well-balanced figure that presents itself as the same on all sides. **Fig. 7**

[8] See note on page 96/97.

Fig. 5

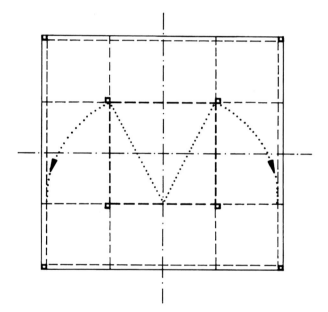

Fig. 6

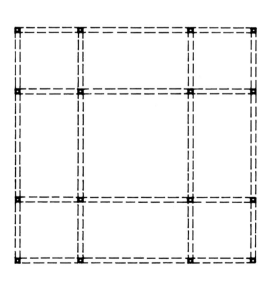

Fig. 7

Fig. 5–9 Plan analysis of the ground floor of the Villa Schwob

Fig. 8

Now that the support positions have been fixed within the initial square the plan figure can expand and "break out" of the rigidity of the square. A field that is clearly defined on both sides limits the outline of the extension and keeps it within an unambiguous *frame*. This frame is also shaped on a basis of geometrical proportionality, which is clearly illustrated in this step. The diagonal of the initial square passes to its bottom line in an arc, and its vertical at this intersection point produces the extension, the frame. This simple geometrical construction for establishing area proportions is based on the I to root 2 proportion, similarly to the Golden Section.[9] The initial square plus the extension field represent this area ratio on both sides. This newly found frame forms the outer limiting line for the semicircular extension figure on both sides; its curve suggests expansion, and thus movement. But it is the straight section between the semicircle and the square, the intermediate piece, that invokes the impression of the expanded figure.

The inner line of the extension is also fixed by the distance between the columns in the centre field. The central point of the radius of the circle can now be fixed on the lateral axis in the proportions of the Golden Section, relating to the previously established external outline. This fixes the distance from the square as the smaller part of the Golden Section. This distance is precisely indicated in Le Corbusier's original plan by the outer lines of a round table and a bed. The outer and inner lines of the outer wall are thus defined geometrically, producing a wall thickness that can be transferred to the other outer walls.

Fig. 9

Transferring the geometrically established wall thickness to the other outside walls means that the outer columns on the outlined square disappear inside these walls. Using light dividing walls to divide off small square side rooms in the corners also blurs the independent load-bearing function of the inner columns. They appear on the surface of the dividing walls in the central space only in some lines. The line of the shallow side-room wings that runs along the street also arises from the outline – the frame – of the rounded side rooms. To this purpose the diagonals of the initial square are extended and intersect with the tangents of the apses, which have also been extended. The intersection points are marked by column positions and provide the outer wall line of the side rooms and the border of the terrace. The "indentation" marking the two entrances is in the form of a staircase wall with its inner wall line at distance A from the line of the initial square. This distance A is derived from the length of the outer zone of the square plus the thickness of the wall.

All the important lines in the Villa Schwob ground plan have now been determined. But how do the "regulating lines", in this case the main diagonal edge relations, affect the façades? Le Corbusier himself has something to say about this in "Towards a New Architecture"[10] with reference to the Villa Schwob, which he thought was his only early work worthy of later publication, on the subject of its façades and their proportional lines of relation: *"Construction of a villa. The general mass of the façades, both front and rear, is based on the same angle, which determines a diagonal whose many parallels and their perpendiculars give the measure for correcting the secondary elements, doors, windows, panels etc., down to the smallest detail. This villa of small dimensions, seen in the midst of other buildings erected without a rule, gives the effect of being more monumental, and of another order."*

[9] The irrational value I to root 2 (equals 1.4142) defines the length of the side in relation to the diagonal of a square. The irrational values of the small and large lengths of the root 2 proportion are:
I : 07071 (minor) and I : 4142 (major).

[10] "Towards a New Architecture", translated by Frederick Etchells, London 1927/99. p. 80

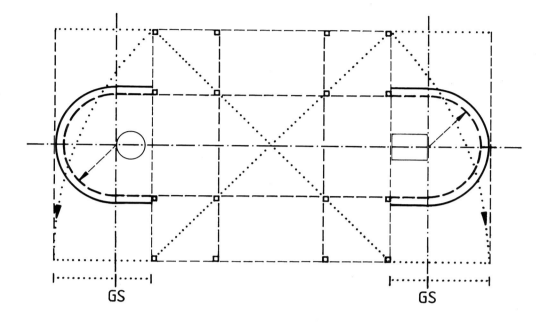

Fig. 8

23

GS   GS

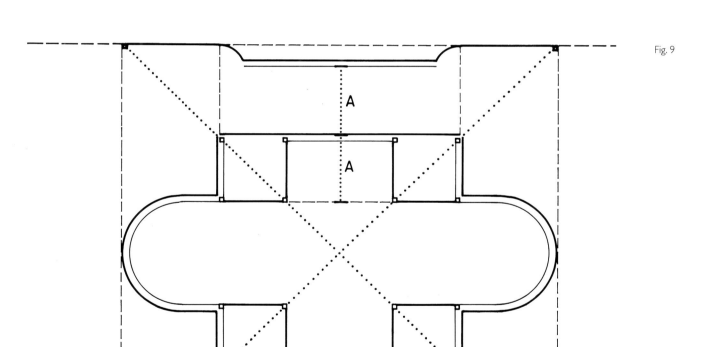

Fig. 9

A

A

The main block means the frontmost section of the building, i. e. the wall of the initial square on the garden side, and the staircase wall on the entrance side. On the two-dimensional plane, both sections form surfaces that stand out clearly in terms of their edges. On the garden side this means the unambiguous overall outline of the protruding section (strong diagonal from top left to bottom right), but on the entrance side a projected set of lines, a relief in the upper part and the inner sides of the two entrance doors in the lower part, separated by a protruding canopy, are to be linked together as a proportional surface figure (again a strong diagonal from top left to bottom right). Here the round canopy columns, which taper towards the top, have their feet planted precisely on an edge. Both surfaces show the ratio of the Golden Section, which has already been discovered in the ground plan, in their short and long sides, one as a horizontal and one as a vertical surface. A large number of reference lines are presented in "Towards a New Architecture", all showing areas in the Golden Section, but all defining partial figures, like windows, for example. Le Corbusier calls this "construction of a villa" in his essay. So it is not the mechanical and technical building process that is the actual act of construction for him, but the intellectual "construction". In this way construction and proportion could almost count as equivalents. *Architecture to me means construction achieved by a trimph of the intellect.*[11] The intention of this book is to show particularly how important proportion was for Le Corbusier as a constructive force and "divine law" when developing designs for his future work.

Figure 10 is an attempt to relate not the façade figures but the essential *building* outlines to each other. The

Main entrance front

geometrical and figurative structure of the building, which is projected in two dimensions here, is based above all on the square (parallel diagonals from bottom left to top right). Unlike the "unambiguous" outline of the Golden Section structure on the garden side, directly comprehensible in its edges, here the structures or part structures are "ambiguous" in thier square proportions and cannot be directly related in their real edge connections. For example, the base point of the rounded section of the building on the left, on the second plane, relates to the point of intersection produced upwards of the large window frame and broad cornice on the front plane at the top (here identified by a diagonal in the left half of the building). It becomes clear that Le Corbusier needs the broad, protruding cornice and its height to make this square relation possible. The front plane of the building also relates to the rear plane of the set-back attic storey: the left-hand lower edge of the protruding body can be placed in a square relationship with the top right protruding plane of the structure on the roof (parallel diagonal in the centre of the section). Another example is that adjacent window outlines are linked visually by square ratios (parallel diagonal in the window on the first floor on the right) and tied into the system of geometrical order.

Relating *layers* is something that crops up a great deal in Le Corbusier's architecture. On the entrance side (see fig. 11) we find – as described above – a Golden Section area ratio bounded by a system of surface lines (diagonal from top left to bottom right). Square area ratios run counter to this (parallel diagonals from bottom left to top right). It is suddenly clear that the empty field above the entrance, previously described in literature as square, is not square at all. In 1950, Rowe described the Villa Schwob as *"compact, coherent and precise"*[12] and places it, particularly in terms of the clenched massiveness of the entrance half, within the aesthetic ideal of the late 18th century. He considers that the empty field above the entrances is the most interesting motif – because it is "modern" – despite a chance that this panel could have been intended for a mosaic or insription.[13] But this attribution of "modernity" certainly has to be seen in the perspective of Brooks' research (see note 2). The frame of this empty field becomes complete to form an imaginary square only below, at the point of intersection with the extension of the top edge of the balustrade of the shallow wings on the right and left (line of dashes). The horde of diagonals of this square field suggests further square proportions of areas of planes layered one behind the other, which are related to each other in this way.

At this stage of the analysis it is possible to assert that in his elevations Le Corbusier fundamentally "conceals"

[11] Willy Boesiger/Oskar Stonorov (ed.), "Le Corbusier. Œuvre complète", vol. 1, Zurich 1929, footnote p. 11.
[12] Colin Rowe, "Mannerism and Modern Architecture", Architectural Review 1950, quoted from "The Mathematics of the Villa and Other Essays", Cambridge, Mass. 1982, p. 30.

[13] Ibid., p. 31.
[14] Incidentally this surface was not intended to remain empty, but to support an artistic design. Brooks proved this conclusively ("Le Corbusier's Formative Years", p. 459).
[15] The original French title is "Vers une architecture", Paris 1922.

Fig. 10
Fig. 11

24

the pure square proportion, as is proved by the example of the square on the entrance side.[14] The opposite is true of Golden Section proportions that are clearly illustrated in outline. It remains to be seen whether this will be an approach taken in principle in the future work.

Le Corbusier's step forwards "Towards a New Architecture"[15] is already to be seen in this work, which is still heterogeneous and hybrid. The Villa Schwob says farewell to a first and important phase of his life, and this leave-taking – emphasized by his departure for Paris while the house was being built – will now be a characteristic feature of Le Corbusier's life on many occasions.

Von Moos[16] provides an apposite analysis of this building in one of the most important early works on Le Corbusier's completed œuvre, "Elements of a Synthesis". He states that Le Corbusier has successfully translated the widest possible variety of contemporary influences into an entirely personal idiom. The result, he goes on to say, is a generous, elegant and stylishly fashionable composition, if somewhat cramped and heterogeneous in its elements.

25

Fig. 10 Garden façade
(Proportion lines drawn in by Klaus-Peter Gast, 1999)

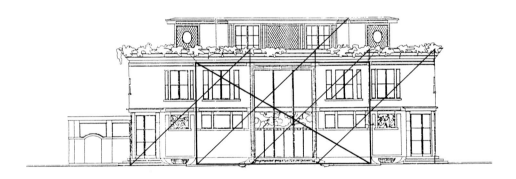

Fig. 11 Entrance façade
(Proportion lines drawn in by Klaus-Peter Gast, 1999)

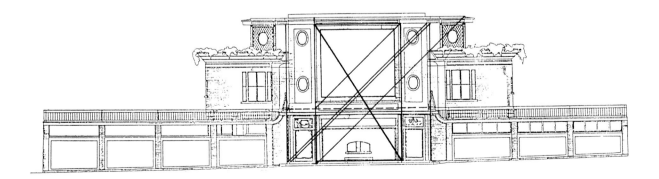

[16] Stanislaus von Moos, "Le Corbusier. Elemente einer Synthese", Stuttgart 1968, pp. 52–53; English edition: "Elements of a Synthesis", Cambridge, Mass. 1979.

The Dom-ino Principle
1914–1916

Fig. 12 In December 1914, Le Corbusier (Jeanneret) made the first sketches for a new constructive but particularly also aesthetic principle for the finding of architectural form, which Eisenman called a *"historical rupture"*,[17] a reference to the resultant view of space – and to another aspect, which will be mentioned later.

Le Corbusier started thinking about these matters when he was still in his home town of La Chaux-de-Fonds. His ideas are based on his experience with reinforced concrete while working with Perret in Paris. He came up with a so-called skeleton construction, in which all the loads and forces produced by gravity are concentrated. The principle had already been applied by predecessors of Le Corbusier: it is no longer necessary to distribute loads evenly throughout all the zones of a building, usually the walls, which means sizing these parts according to the forces involved. It is now possible to concentrate them at a few points. Using the new material of reinforced concrete, in which two materials distribute the forces exerted, those forces can be absorbed by slender columns. But Le Corbusier now takes this an extremely important step further, which was to shape the future of building all over the world: the columns are no longer arranged on the plane of the façade, but set back, and moreover: they are revealed, and shown independently of all interior walls and fittings, thus acquiring an autonomous and therefore architecturally significant character. They are no longer constructional parts born of necessity, but independent elements within a whole that still belong to it and have to be designed. The separation of load-bearing function and cladding function for the outside wall by setting back the columns has extraordinary consequences: the design of the façade becomes almost independent of structural requirements, as a pure covering to keep out the weather. One result of these ideas is the continuous, horizontal band of windows, whose emphatically horizontal quality has its reason precisely in its emergence in this way.

It is possible to say that Le Corbusier had developed this extremely reduced, almost abstract principle because of the necessity for rebuilding and cost reduction associated with the World War, but at the same time he went through his most significant inner transformation, a kind of awakening. His idea of offering a kind of "frame", that can be filled as needed with walls made of any kind of material (for example rubble from build-

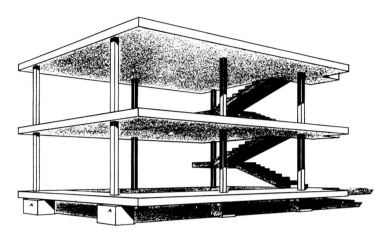

Fig. 12 Dom-ino construction principle, drawing by Le Corbusier

ings damaged in the war), is first of all evidence of a rational mind. The idea of serial manufacture or mass production of parts that are prefabricated or made on the building site points in the same direction. Le Corbusier tried to patent the serial manufacturing process for himself, as he anticipated a high income from mass production, but this was not to be. The name "Dom-ino" also comes from serial manufacture. It is borrowed from the game of dominoes, and involves linking parts that are the same together, in this case whole houses. One feature of dominoes is that the halves of the dominoes with the same number of spots on them are always put down next to each other. Le Corbusier deals with the accumulation of this "building prototype" in the same way, and develops alternative arrangements of the columns that offer the possibility of forming a chain on two sides, similarly to the game of dominoes. The stairs are on one side, and a space that is left open on the other, so that various combinations are possible.

[17] Peter Eisenman, "La Maison Dom-ino and the Self-referential Sign", Oppositions 15/16, 1979, pp. 118–128, also: Rizzoli, New York 1991, p. 22.

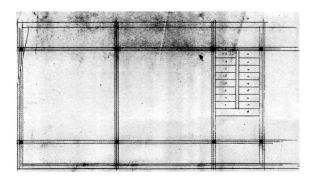

Fig. 13 Dom-ino support structure, drawing by Le Corbusier

Fig. 13 In the ground plan for the Dom-ino *principle* – to focus Eisenman's somewhat too comprehensive definition of the perspective sketch in fig. 12 as "La maison Dom-ino" a little – it is remarkable that the distance between the columns within the usable space is the same in both directions, so that square fields emerge between the columns. The steps are half a field wide, so that within one dom-ino element the distance between the columns in the longitudinal direction produces a rhythm of 1 : 1 : 1/2. Given the predetermined rectangular form and roof slab dimensions of the basic building type, the fact that the columns are set back equally on both sides produces an equal protrusion of the roof in the transverse direction. The lines are continued on the right-hand edge of the drawing as a sign that the building can be extended. A whole variety of ways in which the

Fig. 14 buildings can be linked together are shown in figure 14. The diagram is reduced to the outline of the house and the stairs, and combines variants of the same type as houses with their own plot of land in a conventional estate pattern with street axis, symmetrical groupings, emphasized corners and a square formed to define a centre. The radical element of the Dom-ino concept is completely contradicted here by translation into conventional urban forms. Le Corbusier describes a group of mass-production houses built on the dom-ino principle in "Towards a New Architecture"[18] that are linked together to create a large-scale pattern. It is quite clear here that the individual house is subordinated for the sake of a coherent complex, producing a strongly horizontal structure reduced to two storeys. These houses would be *"capable of being erected by unskilled labor"*[19] and would nevertheless be complete in the shortest possible time. They would be *"concrete houses. The con-*

crete was poured in from above as you would fill a bottle. A house is completed in three days. It comes out of the shuttering like a casting. But this shocks our contemporary architects, who cannot believe in a house that is made in three days …"[20] Clearly the tone suggests a process that is practical and easy to handle; there is no mention of aesthetic categories. Even when the Dom-ino building principle is to be *"applied to a middle-class house"*[21] it tends to be the financial aspects that are emphasized. This produces similarly hybrid forms between abstraction and convention as were realized shortly afterwards in the Villa Schwob. The individual buildings designed by Le Corbusier on the Dom-ino principle turn out to be even more conventional and more committed to a 19th century façade structure than the linked terraced houses. This may reflect Le Corbusier's idea of this period of prestigious appearances as an image of domestic rank. But this is also an indication of the

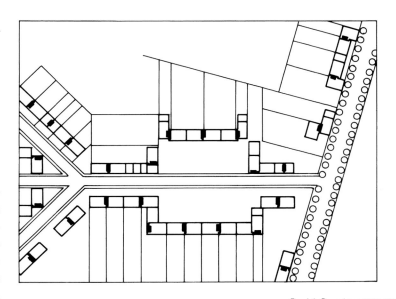

*Fig. 14 Dom-ino estate structure
(redrawn after Le Corbusier by Klaus-Peter Gast, 1999)*

fact that the Dom-ino principle, as the name itself suggests, is able to express its specific quality especially in combining and linking units and the "variations on a theme" associated with this. The serial idea is constitutive for the Dom-ino principle. But this does not establish whether the rationality contained in this idea is essentially functional or aesthetic.

[18] Le Corbusier, "Towards a New Architecture", pp. 230 and 234.
[19] Ibid.
[20] Ibid.
[21] Ibid.

Fig. 15

Fig. 15 shows an upstairs floor in a Dom-ino building. Here we can see how awkwardly Le Corbusier arranges the plan in his early concept. The columns have moved inwards off the plane of the façade, but the resultant advantages – free, independent placing of supports and free façade design – are not exploited, because their consequences have not yet been realized. And the columns also disappear almost completely in the dividing walls relating to the grid, which struggle to work their way round the fixed staircase figure. The back bedroom is a blind room not connected with the landing. Here it is clear that Le Corbusier did not immediately recognize and implement the revolutionary design principles associated with the Dom-ino system. On the contrary, these insights were developed gradually in the various design and development stages via the constraints and disadvantages of a prescribed outline and fixed grids.

The "form" of this basic type, which is not per se a building, is determined by geometry. Geometry fixes the rectangular shape, the cross-section of the columns, the distance between the columns and the relationship of the stairs to "space", first created by the distance between the columns. Geometry also creates the longitudinal dimension of the floor slab, which seem so natural at first sight. The proportion of the Golden Section is involved in setting the freely chosen ratio of width to length of the slab, which is not dependent on any apparent external conditions. It can be assumed that the distance between the floor slabs, in other words the height of each storey, which is difficult to discover because of the perspective of the drawing, also follows certain fixed measurements that are in a carefully calculated ratio to other measurements. Clearly the development of a horizontal quality of the façade is an automatic result of the liberation of the outer wall from its load-bearing function. Thus one façade figure – the strip window – becomes comprehensible in its logical form, which is particular emphasized, indeed celebrated. Le Corbusier was to develop the most far-reaching consequence of this idea, dissolving the whole of the cladding into glass, in his later designs. This is a design principle that has remained valid to the present day, despite its questionable quality.

As can be seen in the drawing in figure 12, all the parts of the Dom-ino are reduced to simple, geometrical figures: the columns, square in cross-section, become slender bodies, the even, horizontally layered floors become flat, precise slabs and the foundations become cubic volumes. Historical formal quotations are completely abandoned: columns without capitals and plinths, ceilings without cornice or frieze, no ornamentation. A staircase, shaded at the back but thus all the more dramatic in its effect, provided with steps that are a solid

28

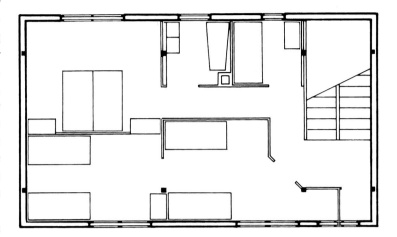

*Fig. 15 Upper storey of a dwelling built on the Dom-ino principle
(redrawn after Le Corbusier by Klaus-Peter Gast, 1999)*

presence on their diagonal slabs, "hangs" freely between the planes. The vertically arranged layering of equal parts (floor slabs in this case), though it is horizontal in its effect, produces an effect of "floating" that had previously been largely unknown. Conventional buildings were rooted in the ground by their density and weight, and their façade, from the heavy rustication at the bottom to the decorated area at the top, expressed their "weight" hierarchically. But in the Dom-ino principle a contradiction that disturbs the eye is introduced: load-bearing elements are reduced to the point of incredibility in their material quality and dimensions, and something that actually is "heavy", the floor level, seems to escape from the ground and float away. A completely new view of these connections, which was not to be completely revealed to Le Corbusier himself until it was translated into concrete designs, means a reversal of the static and constructive ideas for implementing architecture that had prevailed until this time. Something that at first seems to be required as "pure" construction is transformed into an aesthetic norm by being perceived in a new way. Behind the Dom-ino principle, which seems so simple and so plausible, derived from necessary, possibly functional conditions, an aesthetic concept is actually concealed that carries fundamental features of Le Corbusier's work within itself: order, shaped by geometry and proportion, the abstraction of an individualized building or part of a building to form a "prism", a horizontal quality for the façade created by a free covering body running along the protruding floor slabs, and not least: the contradiction between directly plausible structural necessity and the appearance of the building.

Eisenman's[22] acute analysis along these lines shows that the "how" of the perspective sketch of the Dom-ino principle shown (see fig. 12) also follows an unambiguous intention and did not emerge as an automatic product created by constructive or functional conditions. In each case, the figure and its parts appear as a "self-referential sign";[23] it is not until this self-referential, self-fulfilling element is added that architecture is able to emerge within Modernism. This seems correct and meaningful, as Le Corbusier, through his very special subjective selection from various possibilities of form and arrangement of these parts, for example the definition of the floor slab in terms of the Golden Section, has imbued them with a meaning that goes far beyond pragmatic considerations. He has *charged* these principles, as it were.

The Dom-ino principle thus represents an aesthetic innovation of this period that goes well beyond functional or constructive principles.

29

[22] Eisenman, "La Maison Dom-ino …".
[23] "This then may be a primitive though truly Modernist phenomenon, one that speaks about its mere existence and its own condition of being", ibid. p. 29.

Citrohan House
design from 1920
realized 1927   Stuttgart   Germany

By 1920, Charles-Edouard Jeanneret's horizons had been considerably broadened in his new Parisian surroundings. His meeting with Amédée Ozenfant, an artist who was already established in Paris, in 1918 is important in this context. Ozenfant introduced him to the new world of Cubism and subsequently that of Purism, an enormous step for Jeanneret, who until then had been trapped within provincial convention. He was able to take in and process "new" things with astonishing receptivity and speed. This led to radical turns and to saying farewell to fundamental beliefs that had been valid until then. 1920 is also the important year of the new identity: Jeanneret, working with Ozenfant and the poet Paul Dermée, the principal initiator, produced the magazine "L'Esprit Nouveau". In the early stages they all used several different names for their contributions, to make it look as if there were more writers than was in fact the case. It was in this context that Jeanneret adopted the pseudonym "Le Corbusier" – for a specific purpose, and without the artistic pose that is so often described. It derives from an old family name. It was not until readers started wanting to get in touch with this as yet unknown Le Corbusier that the future name was fixed.

The Citrohan House emerged at this time. It is an illustration of this change of identity, as it is the first consistent "purist" architectural figure in Le Corbusier's œuvre in which a convincing innovative concept and the physical components of the architecture go hand in hand. The main thrust of the following description is that contrary to Le Corbusier's practical and functional explanations of this design type it is dominated by a formal and aesthetic concept.

Fig. 16   The rectangular, block-like shape of the first building of the Citrohan type has two longitudinal walls that are presumably almost entirely closed, a two-storey glazed wall on one short side and an external staircase leading to the first floor and an attic floor. Here there is a framework-like structure consisting of supports and beams in the rear section, behind which a recessed volume can be identified. At the front, on the roof, this construction dissolves into a filigree structure, probably made of metal, which follows the outline of the building. It is

Fig. 17   clear from figure 17 that both the staircase, which seems to have been added on, and also the constructive part of the roof combine with the rear outline of the building, the wall of the short side. The partial figures blend

into each other. If one now looks at the plans of the   Fig. 18
ground and first floors, then it is clear that the space is   Fig. 19
divided to form a two-storey living-hall, from which the dining area on the ground floor and a spiral staircase are separated by a cupboard unit and a spiral staircase. Behind this are side rooms for the staff, and the kitchen, which has a separate entrance, and on the first floor a gallery and a bedroom. This confirms the assumption that the longitudinal walls are closed with the exception of a defined zone.

This motif of a room that is unambiguously oriented by a large opening, but also of the building as a whole with closed longitudinal walls and openings concentrated in the rear third, is to be found even in the early Stotzer and Jaquemet Houses in La Chaux-de-Fonds (see fig. 3 and fig. 4), and runs through Le Corbusier's work until 1927, the year in which the only Citrohan type house was actually built. While in the Stotzer and Jaquemet designs the position of the houses on a slope with a view of the surrounding landscape require large openings, here, in figures 16 and 17, the motif of unambiguous orientation is taken over by the almost complete glazing of one side, but it is done for a different purpose. It is no longer intended for looking out, in other words extroverted, but for bringing in light, and also for admitting the public space, and so a means of introverting the public. Privacy is restricted in favour of a more intensive relationship of the outside to the inside. The eye falls on the living-space, the interior, in which activity takes place and in which we find the arrangement of the composed sections, so carefully harmonized with each other. It seems reasonable to assume that Le Corbusier did not intend the undue abundance of light to be mainly for the benefit of the residents, but was more concerned to shift the space with its proportions and the disposition of the figures that make it up "into the right light". An excess of light can be unpleasant, indeed painful. The size of the living-room does not necessarily demand a window of this size, and so here another motif can be adduced as a cause, and it is one that seems to have fixed itself in Le Corbusier's mind: the studio window. The studio has played a large part since the start of his contact with Ozenfant 1918. It needs a specific light for painting and thus for the painter to feel good, and Le Corbusier was specially aware of this as he put a great deal of energy into painting during this period. The painter's very special needs for an evenly lit space are now transferred to a residential building as a studio motif. The two-storey residential hall with double glazing on the garden side is also to be found in the Villa Schwob (see fig. 10), there more as a symbol of generosity, relaxation and luxury. But it remains doubtful whether this bourgeois motif of enjoying life in a re-

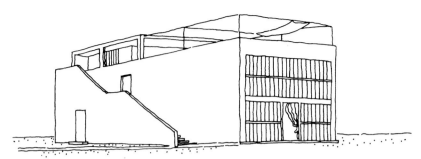

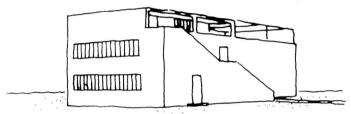

laxed and meditative fashion – many of the accessories in his drawing, like armchairs, coffee service and open books confirm this idealized feeling for life – can be transferred to a house for the so-called man in the street. With all this restriction of privacy and living in the countryside with a hedonistic attitude, Le Corbusier had succumbed to a dream that did not in any way correspond with reality, especially in these post-war days. Le Corbusier was not able to realize this dream until later, but for clients who were as different as it is possible to be.

As Huse[24] probably rightly comments, Le Corbusier's description of the discovery of a two-storey living-room with large-scale glazing on one side has been raised to the scope of myth. Here are Le Corbusier's own words: "We eat in a coachmen's café in the centre of Paris: there is a bar, and behind that the kitchen; a suspended ceiling divides the interior into two vertically, a shop-window opens on to the street. We discovered this one day and remarked that here was everything needed for a complete architectural mechanism, and it could also be used to organize a home. Simplified light sources; a single large opening at each end; two stone load-bearing walls at the sides, a flat roof on top; a veritable box that could be used as a house."[25] According to von Moos,[26] this was the bistrot "Legrende", opposite Ozenfant's studio, later the Café Mauroy, in which Le Corbusier and Ozenfant often used to eat.

But the large opening of the living-hall must be considered especially from formal and aesthetic points of view and related to the above-mentioned cubature of the building as a whole (see fig. 16). Le Corbusier suggests this himself by not illustrating the view of the building frontally, but by showing it in an especially favourable diagonal perspective to illustrate his design intentions.

Here it becomes clear that the probably rectangular glazing, which almost entirely dissolves the wall of the narrow side, represents an independent figure that forms a contrast with the closed area of the longitudinal wall. The corner solution with its succinct outline creates a vertical symmetrical axis that is "closed" on the left (light-coloured field) and open on the right (hatched field). This motif of a contrast between light-coloured solid sections and dark window area with clearly marked outlines, with the proportions – i. e. the edges of surface figures related to each other – carefully harmonized with each other, dominates façade composition until the early thirties.

The opening of the "box" on two sides indicated by Le Corbusier in his description finds a significant form in this first design for the Citrohan house type (see fig. 17): the long window, also called strip or continuous window. A striking feature here is its even division using vertical bars, a motif adopted by Le Corbusier from his years of work on slaughterhouses in Paris. His slaughterhouse designs are important, as their industrial character brings together all the elements of the later Citrohan for the first time, like for example the prismatic cubature and the long window. The horizontal quality of the long window allows the horizontal layering from the previously designed Dom-ino principle to appear clearly in the façade: the building is divided into horizontal layers, but without breaking apart or showing signs of instability. The "complementary" volume of the staircase at the side and the closed wall of the structure on the roof fix the divided mass of the rear wall. Here too the way in which this perspective sketch is presented is important: the corner view over the diagonal emphasizes the volume formed by "smoothing": various individual parts blend together to form a new and homogeneous whole. This makes it possible to

[24] Huse, "Le Corbusier", p. 36.
[25] Boesiger/Stonorov (ed.), "Le Corbusier. Œuvre complète", vol. I, p. 31: "Nous mangions dans un petit restaurant de cochers, du centre de Paris; il y a le bar (le zink), la cuisine au fond; une soupente coupe en deux la hauteur du local; la devanture ouvre sur la rue. Un beau jour, on découvre cela et l'on s'aperçoit que les preuves sont ici présentes, de tout un mécanisme

architectural qui peut correspondre à l'organisation de la maison d'un homme. Simplification des sources lumineuses: une seule grande baie à chaque extrémité; deus murs portants latéraux; un toit plat dessus; une véritable boîte qui peut être utilement une maison."
[26] Von Moos, "Le Corbusier", p. 93.

view the parts and the whole in two ways, and creates a form that is consciously contradictory. The staircase is no longer suspended, but suddenly becomes part of the rear wall, which again encloses the long narrow building and seems to be cut out diagonally, following the line of the stairs.

Le Corbusier toyed with the idea of producing the Citrohan series type in large quantities, *"a house like a motor-car"*.[27] Linking up with the Dom-ino principle that had previously been developed, which promised great freedoms in the design of this house type, many variants could be developed, although only one was to be realized at a late stage. But the Dom-ino principle is not applied with sufficient consistency. Even this first Citrohan design, in which it is latently present, does not show the inherent advantages of this pioneering construction system. Even so: the possible existence of the skeleton system, absorbed into the outer walls, can be read in the structurally arranged columns at roof level. This could be a suggestion of the concealed system of reinforced concrete columns. In "Towards a New Architecture", Le Corbusier describes his Citrohan design as *"conceived and carried out like an omnibus or a ship's cabin … We must fight against the old-world houses, which made a bad use of space. We must look upon the house as a machine for living in or as a tool"*.[28] These sentences are as famous as they are misunderstood. Like the whole essay, they are mere polemic. The crucial feature of "Towards a New Architecture" is the provocative and subversive element, the intention to shock and make people open their eyes. In order to do this, Le Corbusier used concepts and images that absolutely do not fit in with the idea of the "house", on the contrary, he uses metaphors that invoke other associations. These almost Dada-esque juxtapositions (the Parthenon and a sports car) are a means of reinforcing the statement, which raises the intensity of the writing's impact – even at the risk of being misunderstood. Provocation forces reflection. This is where the success of this essay lies. But if one looks at an omnibus or a ship's cabin dating from those days, there are no similarities in either functional or formal terms! The commercial aspect does not hold either, as the Citrohan house realized on the Weissenhof estate in Stuttgart was one of the most expensive contributions to the exhibition. There is no doubt that the markedly extravagant use of space in early architecture applies to the Citrohan design: there is no comparison between the way in which the side rooms are cramped together and the excessively large living-hall, which is so expensive to heat. And Le Corbusier's absurdly exaggeratedly scaled interior perspectives for even the smallest of connected spaces, the enlargement of normally scaled

spaces into something immeasurable contradicts his written statements. The aim of this approach is to establish a key feature that seems to be important, indeed inevitable to Le Corbusier for the future, and he was to be proved right about this: industrial manufacture. The construction method for buildings was to come close to the images of omnibus and ship's cabin that he used, and was to differ radically from the individually crafted single edition that had previously been the norm. And it is mainly here that the core of these associative comparisons lies. A building was to be made industrially in just the same way as a machine, and this is the correct context for the "machine à habiter". Of course this paradoxical combination of concepts was carefully chosen as well, to invoke the alienation effect described above: neither the aesthetics of the apparatus nor the technical and precise function of a machine was to be directly applied to the building, as even the simple Citrohan house type shows that criteria quite other than those of pure function are to the fore. The concept of the "machine à habiter" is certainly one of the most frequently misinterpreted metaphors in 20th-century architecture.

Defects are quickly evident if one looks at the functional context of his design concept. There is an entrance without a preparatory zone as a porch or hallway. It leads directly in to the large living-room and would have to be treated as something like a French window. As well as this there is another entrance that quite clearly serves only the kitchen, and thus cannot be seen as the main entrance. It is certainly possible to reach the first floor via an internal spiral staircase, but the terrace level is accessible only via the exterior staircase, which is not protected from the rain. All this is more reminiscent of a holiday home in the south than a standard dwelling intended for mass production. As well as this, it is not clear where the shape of a narrow rectangle as the ideal for a house comes from, as neither functional nor local conditions suggest it. Even the two-storey living area does not require a building in this form, as the two-storey quality can effortlessly be created in other configurations. A house that stands isolated in the landscape – and this is the requirement as formulated – tends to need concentricity or a universal orientation, as can be seen in its most extreme form in Palladio's Villa Capra "La Rotonda", rather than linear orientation on one or two sides, which is more suited to an infill building in a densely populated area. And whether the organization and form of a Parisian transport café provides an adequate answer is extremely doubtful. A far more likely justification is that the figure of the long, narrow block itself played the crucial part: a prism set in the landscape, something that was fascinating to Le

Fig. 18
Fig. 19

[27] Le Corbusier, "Towards a New Architecture", p. 240.
[28] Ibid.

Fig. 18

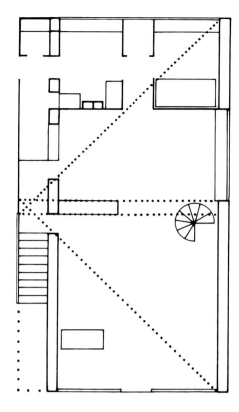

Fig. 19

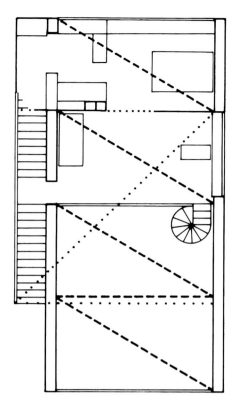

33

*Fig. 18 and 19 Proportional plan figures
(redrawn after Le Corbusier by Klaus-Peter Gast, 1999)*

Corbusier. Form "as such" is presented, *"a self-referential sign"* (Eisenman[29]), the pure body in sharp outline as a contrast with nature and in celebration of itself as a sculpture. This also makes it possible to understand the above-mentioned blending of the staircase, the main volume and the structures on the roof: a sculptural process is contained within the act of fitting different parts together and making them homogeneous inside a continuous surface consisting of the same material. This is to say that Le Corbusier perceives the form of the Citrohan type as *a free definition*. It reflects an individual decision to exist as an autonomous figure. It is an idealized determination of form, the finding of an archaic figure that knows only *one* pre-existence and *one* model in the sense of an idea: geometry. A rational element of justification is to be found in the geometrical form chosen – proportion, for example – but this does not reveal the decision-making process or even the actual idea behind the design.

Clear geometrical figures can be identified in the ground plans shown, i. e. areas whose edge can be related to each other geometrically. They do not "prove" the origins of the long, narrow building, but they do explain its final, defined form. On the ground floor (see fig. 18) two overlapping squares can be constructed. Their outer lines determine the position of the narrow

sides and thus the length of the building. These squares include the breadth of the external steps, but there has to be an imaginary completion of the steps to the front edge, to the glass façade. Thus the stairs are not a mere appendage, but an integral part of the main volume, as already described above in relation to the rear view (see fig. 17). But the overlapping double square borders only on the inner line of one longitudinal wall. Thus the internal and external outlines are related to each other that "actually", in reality, cannot be seen together. Le Corbusier marks the overlapping of the two squares in the ground plan, so that their actual existence in the genesis of the design can be seen as definite: the outlines of a piece of furniture, probably a cupboard unit, follow the overlapping width precisely, and the spiral staircase impinges upon a trace as well.

The first floor as a gallery level shows another important geometrical figuration. Le Corbusier gains a specific sense of interior proportion by dividing the space as a whole into "tracks" oriented to unambiguous interior edges, while the aerial space in the living-room is made up of two of these zones. To do this, four zones are arranged together in proportions of the Golden Section in each case. Here the proportional figure of the Golden Section is allocated to spatial relations that can be perceived and understood by the viewer, for exam-

[29] Eisenman, "La Maison Dom-ino ...".

ple to the point at which the longitudinal wall and the window intersect at the back and to the intersection of one dividing wall with the window and the longitudinal wall. In addition to this a centrally placed square relates the border of the flight of stairs to the outlines of rooms.

34

View from the street shortly after completion

Entrance side with two-storey living-room window

There are a number of variants on the Citrohan house.[30] We shall now take a short look at the Citrohan model that actually was built in Weissenhof, Stuttgart, as a contrast with the first conceptual design, which has been discussed above and defines the characteristics of this type of house.[31]

Fig. 20
Fig. 21

The ground floor plan is already considerably different from the first type, as only a restricted zone of the building is on the access level. The rest of the area is empty and bordered by columns that carry the complete volume above them. The ground floor provides access via the stairs, a boiler-room and various side rooms. The plan figure gives the impression that the outline, like a garment that has shrunk, has pulled back from the actual outline of the building. This contrasts with the curved sections, which tend more to suggest that it has been extended. Here free play around a fixed arrangement of columns – the Dom-ino principle – is presented as a suggestive movement. The first floor as the actual living level is the same as the first type in principle, but there are changed proportions in the outline as a whole and emphasized dividing walls with especially fluent curves. The gallery level above this (broken lines) runs diagonally, a fireplace cupboard sculpture divides the living-room from the dining area

Rear façades

---

[30] At the Institut für Baugeschichte, Prof. Thies, University of Braunschweig, Ingo Schrade, Frankfurt and the author carried out extensive, detailed analyses of the Citrohan House 1009, a variant on the house type used in Stuttgart. These confirm the results presented above.

[31] A detailed and sometimes amusing account of Le Corbusier's designs in Stuttgart during the building period appears in Roth's brochure for the opening of Werkbund exhibition: Alfred Roth, "Zwei Wohnhäuser von Le Corbusier and Pierre Jeanneret", Akad. Verlag Dr. Wedekind, Stuttgart 1927 and Krämer Verlag, Stuttgart 1977.

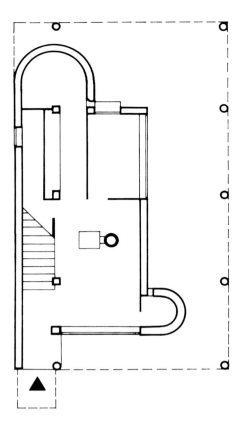

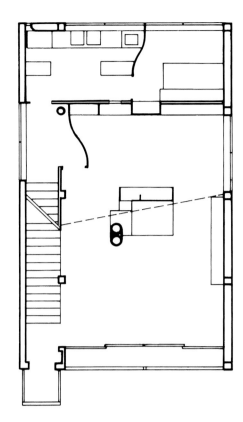

Fig. 20 Access level in the Citrohan house in Weissenhof, Stuttgart
(redrawn after Le Corbusier by Klaus-Peter Gast, 1999)

Fig. 21 Living level in the Citrohan house in Weissenhof, Stuttgart
(redrawn after Le Corbusier by Klaus-Peter Gast, 1999)

and the stairs are now an integral part of the main volume – and the access problem is solved. There is no question that the Citrohan serial type has reached its most mature phase here.

Fig. 22
Fig. 23
Of particular interest in this context is Le Corbusier's orientation to geometrical and proportional reference figures that define the outlines and dimensions of interiors. In figure 22 it becomes clear that the overall ground plan figure in its external line, including the curves, is inscribed in the frame of a double square (dotted diagonals). In contrast with this, almost all the outlines and interior dimensions are dominated by the proportions of the Golden Section (bold broken diagonals). Even the store-room has these proportions. Thus the question arises of whether the overall proportions are determined by this ratio as well. On the first floor – two broken parallel diagonals identify the edges of the outline as a whole – the inner and outer lines of the longitudinal walls relate to each other in the proportion of the Golden Section. This produces a powerfully oscillating element: the above-mentioned diagonals seem to fluctuate around a defined distance – the space produced by the two layers of the glazing and behind by the space created by the depth of the row of kitchen fittings – producing a shift. At the so-called "place of the right angle",[32] it is possible to make

out a line – broken here – running vertically to the main diagonal, which fixes the spatial outline of the dining area, also in the Golden Section. As in the first Citrohan type, here too a double square can be inscribed into the general outline (dotted diagonals). This time the staircase is not included. But the fact that this geometrical figure actually does have a part to play in determining the width of the stairs is proved by the "intermediate piece" of the double square, the support integrated into the wall that can be seen opposite as an outline in the interior space.

The free definition of the form of the rectangularly oriented volume on the basis of geometrical premises can therefore be assumed in precisely the same way for the Stuttgart Citrohan type as well. But there is another regulator of scale apart from this which, derived from function, helps crucially to determine the dimensions of the building: the window as a module, or put more precisely, the sliding window for which Le Corbusier applied for a patent. Reichlin[33] shows that the new, precisely manufactured industrial window was seen here as a symbol of technical progress and considered to be a demonstration object at this showpiece in the form of an internationally acclaimed exhibition. The window consists of a double sliding element and is used on all four sides of the building in a range of variations, i. e.

Fig. 24
Fig. 25

[32] Le Corbusier, "Le Modulor", Paris 1950, p. 26; engl. edition: "The Modulor", London 1954.

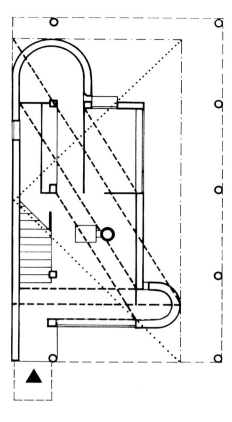 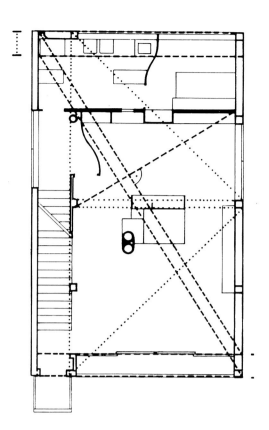

Fig. 22 and 23 Proportional plan figures for the access and living levels (redrawn after Le Corbusier by Klaus-Peter Gast, 1999)

combinations. These openings explain the structure of the building, the position of the storeys and the breadth of the space. They are immediately intelligible on the outside, the distance between the columns seems to derive from the window module – an entirely functional matter seems to be going into practice here. And yet something else is conveyed as well: the window arranges and divides areas of the façades into a game of positives and negatives. The surface figures of the façades based on the edges of the windows are directly linked geometrically, even in the third dimension. This is clear in the simultaneous consideration of the short and long sides (see figs. 25 and 24). On the main side, the short façade with a great deal of glazing, the window dissolves the volume almost completely; only a small strip on the left and at the top remains solid. The long side has a large white area of about the same size on the side that connects directly with the glass façade, bordered by two individual adjacent double windows on the right and the roof garden above. The dissolved short side and the closed long side form a complementary figure along the diagonal, producing a puzzle picture of open and closed bodies. And the three windows of the same kind on the long side (see fig. 24), which are "layered" one above the other, form what is essentially an open zone in contrast with the closed

white area of the same size that is immediately adjacent. The major dissolution of precise areas within a precise body outline, made possible by reinforced concrete, produces some surreal effects: on the ground floor, which shifts backwards, the volume is completed only on one side as a wall, it stands on this wall slab, so to speak, and has to be kept from falling down by a support element on the right. The roof garden beam, which completes the outline of the prism, floats in the air as a part of the building that actually is heavy without any clearly emphasized constructive support.

Neither the Dom-ino principle nor Le Corbusier's "Five Points Towards a New Architecture", which will be further examined later and were first published in connection with the building in Stuttgart, is applied here consistently. As usual, Le Corbusier's theory runs counter to his built practice. However, this does not necessarily mean that the theory is questionable.
But in this context, concerning the question of the special quality and the weight of Le Corbusier's kind of rationality, Wedepohl's criticism[34] in 1927 hits upon a relevant contradiction relating to Le Corbusier's distance from the Stuttgart exhibition's claim of "subsistence level" housing: *"If the type of dwelling is intended to be appropriate to the type of person, then the only occupant*

[33] Bruno Reichlin, "The Single-Family Dwelling of Le Corbusier and Pierre Jeanneret at the Weissenhof", in "In the Footsteps of Le Corbusier", New York 1991, pp. 37–57.
[34] Edgar Wedepohl, "Die Weißenhofsiedlung der Werkbundausstellung 'Die Wohnung' in Stuttgart 1927, Wasmuths Monatshefte für Baukunst XI 1927, p. 396 ff.

38

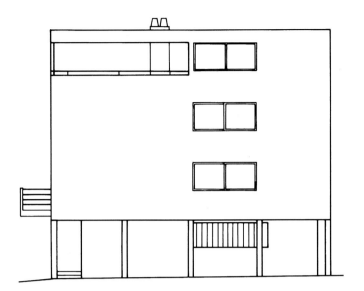

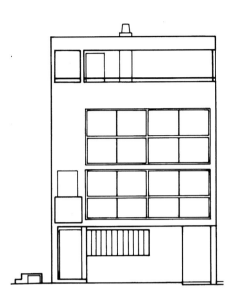

Fig. 24 East elevation (redrawn after Le Corbusier by Klaus-Peter Gast, 1999)

Fig. 25 Sough elevation (redrawn after Le Corbusier by Klaus-Peter Gast, 1999)

one could think of for houses of the Corbusier type would be a certain kind of intellectual... unencumbered by historical ballast, unsentimental, generous and homeless, detaching himself from all conditions, and who would perhaps like to live in this nomad's tent made of iron and concrete, which despite its material hardness is not firmly and heavily growing into and rooted with the earth, not a part of the native soil... Certainly the intellectual is a form of modern man, but is he the type whose demands and needs should determine the form that built housing should take?"

Villa Besnus
1923   Vaucresson near Paris   France

In 1922, George Besnus, after visiting the Salon de l'Automne, approached Le Corbusier to order a house similar to the Maison Citrohan, which had been presented there. After visiting various sites with Le Corbusier they chose a plot in Vaucresson, a suburb of Paris, placed on a ridge about one storey high on the street side.

Le Corbusier rapidly drew the basic concept, without variants, of a rectangular block parallel with the street with a staircase attached. Here the change of level in the site is used functionally. A ground floor at street level contains the main entrance, the garage and side rooms, and a ground floor on the garden level – set a level higher – becomes the living and working area. Above these are the bedrooms with an internal bathroom. Besnus originally wanted a two-storey studio room as in the Citrohan design, but Le Corbusier developed a single-story room glazed to the ceiling, probably for reasons of the better hierarchical order of the functional areas per floor. In fact he produced a design that has next to nothing in common with the basic Citrohan type, even though the client referred to it expressly and Le Corbusier must have been delighted to have an opportunity of realizing this theoretical model. The plot also seemed extraordinarily well suited, especially as there was a Citrohan variant placed on a ridge, and so this set of conditions had already been considered for a design. So far we have no idea why a design was created that departed from this completely and was absolutely not appropriate to the Citrohan model in its complex basic substance. The only possible assumptions about this would also have to include estimated costs, for example. Le Corbusier does mention implementing his work to date on the free plan when speaking of this design, but even the completely new Dom-ino principles formulated in 1914, the separation of the supporting structure and outer envelope, were not applied in any particular. It is quite clear that no synthesis of these very important thoughts took place at the time.

Besnus was an accommodating man, very open to Le Corbusier's ideas, indeed pretty well an ideal client, who immediately agreed to the smaller studio and very much welcomed the overall concept of the house – the first consistently purist design that was ready to be realized. It is therefore all the more astonishing that very shortly indeed after completion of the building technical defects started to occur, the cellar was constantly flooded, a large crack suggested inadequate foundations, and Le

Main entrance side from the road in the original condition

View from the street with entrance roofing

for example). The repetitive quality of window elements and divisions also suggests an industrial building standard – and masks the fact that the appearance of "serial manufacture" had to be laboriously created by hand. This almost completely symmetrical building rejects functionalist design principles of directly mirroring interior functional hierarchies in the façade. The plan solution of the "whole" makes it possible to produce a façade image that makes itself independent, that does not represent the "interior" as a series of uses but the "exterior" as an ordering principle. The façade becomes *autonomous*. It obeys higher rules of its own. Here symmetry becomes a kind of "ordering anchor", an element that establishes and fixes the building volume with its outer covering, while free figurations flow in the interior. Here the – entirely intentional, and thus very deliberately staged – contradiction between internal "movement" and outward rigidity is clearly revealed.

Fig. 26

Corbusier showed absolutely no interest in paying adequate attention to his first piece of work in a new aesthetic category.

The basic concept of the house is that of the studio room. Here it mutates into a continuous living area containing no closed parts, i. e. it is not divided up by walls with doors in them. The outline of the "open-plan room" can clearly be seen and understood when walking around on this floor. It is "interrupted" only by a wall thrusting into the room with a fireplace sculpture on the end of it, which screens off a kind of entrance from the rest of the area. This room represents the centre of the house. The plan develops from here. It symmetrical glazing, as high as the room, projects the axis outwards, together with two corbels and the strip windows of the same width in the upper storey arranged above them. This almost overpowering and thus surprising symmetry, which Le Corbusier had already overcome in the Citrohan house, is intended to represent the "integrity" of the space and thus of the volume on the outside, despite the fact that there are side rooms like the kitchen behind the closed sections of the walls. The street façade is also markedly symmetrical, even though asymmetry is intended to be conveyed by the inequality of windows on the residential level. And so it can be said that the outside of the house is not so much a programme for demonstrating a principle or system as the Citrohan type was, but rather a mere copy of a formal and aesthetic standard. Undecorated white rendered areas within clear, geometrically defined edges with openings cut into them that relate to each other and dark metal framing as a contrasting play of dark areas on a light ground constitute a repertoire of combinations already well-known at this time (from Loos's work,

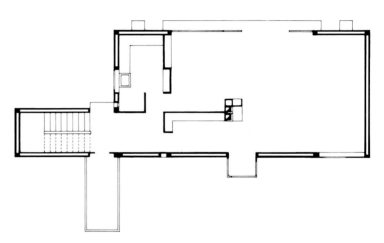

*Fig. 26 Living level with access to garden
(redrawn after Le Corbusier by Klaus-Peter Gast, 1999)*

Von Moos[35] points out the picture-like order of the façade, identifying its individuality in the sense of inner form. A remarkable element additionally emphasizes this individual quality and at the same time raises new questions: a narrow protruding cornice functions as upper conclusion to the building, like a roof slab. Obviously Le Corbusier is referring to historical models in which the façade structure is demonstrated as a vertical hierarchy – base, body and roof; this might constitute a correcting element in the context of geometrical calculation.

Much more important for this façade, and ultimately for the design as a whole, is one element in the role of an independent volume, which was in a different position in the first design: the staircase. It was originally placed vertically to the façade, and in a moment of inspiration Le Corbusier shifted its position to follow the façade.

35 Von Moos, "Le Corbusier", p. 107.

This extends the aspect of the façade by a completely monochrome white area, unblemished and without apertures, separated from the main volume by a glazed joint in the same position as the landing of the staircase inside. Instead of the staircase placed at right angles, an entrance canopy the same length as the stairs is put in place, protruding as a slab and supported by filigree round columns. The entrance canopy is given a corporeal quality as a balcony with metal balustrade and round columns. This produces a contrast between the filigree, dissolved body, the staircase cube and the protruding, completely closed balcony on the axis of the central space. These structures represent three-dimensional projections in front of an overall façade that is emphatically two-dimensional.

In contrast with the house itself, the staircase does not have a cornice and thus detaches itself all the more firmly. The glass joint and constructional parts associated with it are set back as well, so that the separation seems entirely deliberate. And yet the staircase block follows the line of the building and is intended to be seen as "in line" with it, and thus a coherent part. We are now in a position to recognize the autonomous significance of this element, which is isolated in such a contradictory way and at the same time attached to the main volume. The precisely cut cube, without apertures or ornamentation, is a self-referential sign, a merely purist structure, an ideal, a "prisme pur", a work of art.

View from the garden

Staircase area with garden access

The staircase of this little house in Vaucresson is the self-referential leitmotif of this period. Von Moos[36] also refers to the element of separation in this body and asserts that a motif of Modernism and post-Modernism is being expressed at a very early stage here. This was to take the form of a slogan in Louis I. Kahn's later term "servant and served spaces", in other words spaces that are ordered hierarchically. The comparison seems entirely justified, especially as, similarly to Kahn, hierarchy is established – the staircase section serves the main section – but at the same time it is concealed again by being included in the overall outline. Whether the direct establishment of hierarchies will turn out to be a principle of Le Corbusier's designs remains to be seen. The "tracés régulateurs", the regulating surface figures of defined proportion and their diagonals determine the composition of the façade. The extent to which the ground plan was also developed on geometrical principles will be the subject of the following plan analysis, a sequence illustrating the essential structure of the genesis of the design. Before this, Le Corbusier himself should have his say, giving us his own assessment of the

36 Ibid.

Besnus design: "*Practical consequences of the exhibition of urbanism at the Salon d'Automne 1922. It was the moment when all the difficulties manifested themselves at once. In 'L'Esprit Nouveau' theories and viewpoints were proposed for clearing up terrain. In this small house, on the other hand, the problem was to create architecturally: the method of construction as well as efficient solutions for the roofing, window frames, cornices, etc. The 'free plan' was discovered (placing the bathroom at center of the floor plan). Both the window form and its module were defined (height exactly proportioned to the human scale etc.)...*"[37]

42

Present condition of the short side with the staircase section on the right

[37] Boesiger/Stonorov (ed.), "Le Corbusier. Œuvre complète", vol. 1, pp. 48–52.

Present condition of the main entrance side

Position of the building in its present condition

The following analysis refers to the plan of the garden storey.

Fig. 27   The starting-point of the design is a double square of a defined size. It establishes the essentials of the outline of the main section of the building. The geometrical figure of the double square provides a vertical axis (on the plane of the drawing). This is the main symmetrical axis of the building figure and creates a dominant regulating line.

Fig. 28   The double square does not define the precise external outline of the building on all sides. A wall thickness of a defined size dependent on the selected breadth of a supporting column is projected inwards in the upper corners of the double square. This wall thickness is formed by a double-skinned wall slab. Thus the lower line of the double square defines the *outer* trace of the inner wall. As in earlier designs the precise outline of the square and here of the double square is concealed in its character as a significant geometrical proposition.

Fig. 29   The internal line of the blurred double square derived from the breadth of the support – and thus the breadth of the wall – represents the outline of the whole interior. And yet the outline of the original double square, and here especially of half of it, the single square, is the key to the further geometrical development of the ground plan figure. This outline is not immediately visible. The diagonal of half the square, with an arc of a circle produced to the bottom line, generates the area proportions of the Golden Section at the point of intersection. When this intersection point is reflected across the central axis the whole figure is divided into a central area and two flanking zones on the right and left.

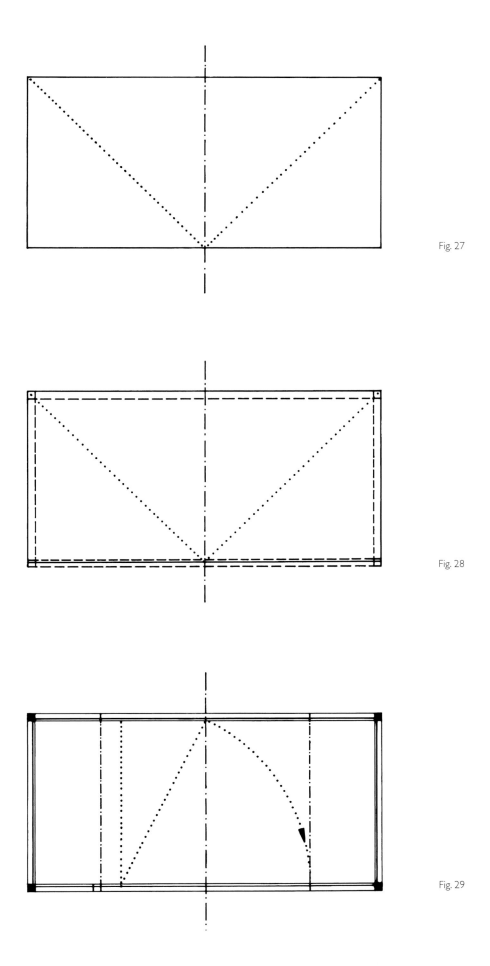

Fig. 27

Fig. 28

Fig. 29

Fig. 27–32 Plan analysis of the living-room floor of the Villa Besnus

Fig. 30

The Golden Section area figure (thick broken diagonal) can be represented intelligibly in the body of the building. The outline of this area defines four more support positions, which clearly define the central space as the main living-room. But here too it is not precisely effective in the interior, because of its dependence on the blurred double square. As the double wall exists on all sides, this ratio of areas "oscillates" by the dimension of the inner wall. And yet it is absolutely clear that Le Corbusier is interested in this proportion relating to the interior space and uses it to establish outlines within the structure of the plan.

The distance between the inner columns, applied to the short side of the building, produces a new central square. With its outline it is possible to define the outline of a volume set centrally above the axis and projecting outwards – as a closed balcony. The square ties this figure into the interior space. On the upper outside line, the distance between the internal columns, at the same time the aperture width of the studio window, clearly relates to the axis of symmetry. In the left-hand outer zone the proportion of the Golden Section can be used to define a line that gives the outline of the kitchen and an important dimension of apertures in the outside wall below it.

46

Fig. 31 This step makes it possible to define the outline of the staircase geometrically. The order for the sequence representing the emergence of the design that we have chosen is thus confirmed, as it is not possible to find a border for the staircase section until after the imaginary square from fig. 30 has been fixed to define the centrally placed balcony cube, and then by doubling this. Here the centre is formed by the axis of the dividing wall with the kitchen, around which the actual wall turns. The width of the staircase is determined by the width of the opening already established as a result of the kitchen. Thus the width of the staircase is taken into the open-plan room, forming an entrance zone there extending to the central axis and a fireplace/shelving sculpture that ends there. The length of the flight of stairs is limited by a Golden Section proportion: the inner line of the staircase to the outer line of its wall. The distance from the house thus emerges in the shape of a platform and a way out to the garden.

All the important lines in the ground plan have now been geometrically determined. What remains to be considered is the canopy over the entrance, which is important for the longitudinal façade. As described above, it emerges, in its unusual balcony function, as a structure that is transparent and yet has a corporal quality. It is derived from a point of intersection between the extended platform line and a Golden Section diagonal which is extended laterally by the width of a column. It becomes clear that the length of the entrance canopy is also reflected in the length of the staircase section of the building.

Fig. 32

The structure of this first purist design by Le Corbusier to be built after the L'Esprit Nouveau pavilion and the Atelier Ozenfant, which is roughly contemporary, is clearly shaped by its inherent order. Starting from a symmetry that is quite evidently present, which can be counted as a "calming" basic structure and at the same time as a classical reminiscence, the interior spaces are determined by proportional area figures. The asymmetrically placed staircase section and the entrance façade work against the symmetry, but they too remain within the ordering structure, which is made up of clear referential lines. The decisive factor is that in this way all the parts of the design, interiors, external lines and façades are bound into a "system" of order.

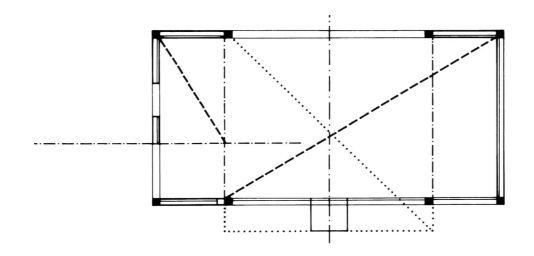

Fig. 30

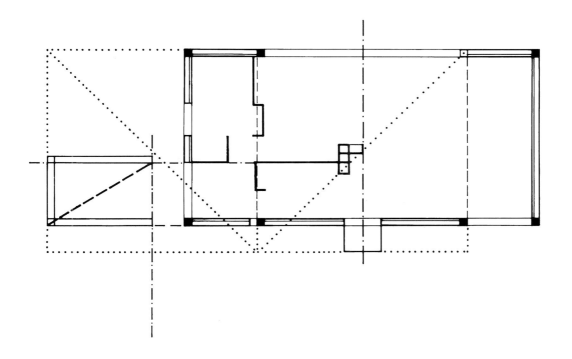

Fig. 31

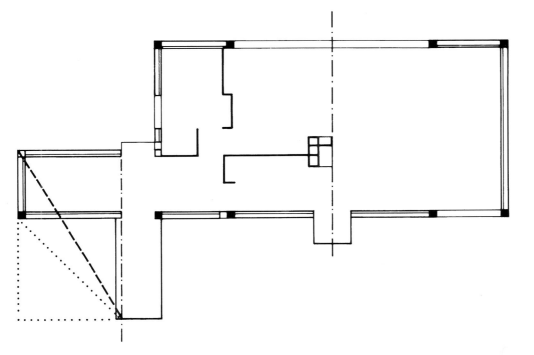

Fig. 32

Villa Stein/de Monzie
1927   Garches/Vaucresson near Paris
France

The American married couple Michael and Sarah Stein and Gabrielle de Monzie jointly commissioned Le Corbusier to built a lavish villa outside greater Paris. Le Corbusier's astonishing links with the affluent Parisian classes made it possible to realize this very important design. Michael Stein, brother of the well-known poet and writer Gertrude Stein, was an art collector and his wife a painter, Madame de Monzie was wealthy and lived alone with her daughter. We do not know quite how the two parties lived together in a way that made it possible to finance the villa. We do know that Gabrielle de Monzie bought the plot in Garches and was officially the client as far as Le Corbusier was concerned. But the house was sold as early as 1935.

The building was placed in the middle of a narrow, very long plot. The design went through numerous variants before the final figure was established.[38] This account will be based on the final version.

When looking at the plans of the ground floor as the access level and the first floor as the main living area, the striking feature alongside the extraordinary generosity of the rooms is the handling of their outlines, which is still very unconventional, and was extremely innovative for the time when they were created. This is undoubtedly a luxury villa, with a hall entrance and a piano nobile as the main floor, which becomes distinct from the ground floor in the rear façade, at which point the latter is set back. Given this approach, the Villa Stein is in a series that could be called classical and seems, as von Moos[39] remarks in general, to be trying to bring together a contrast between classicism and modernism. But these characteristics point towards yet another circumstance: it becomes clear that the clients were also very generous in their intellectual attitude and as far as can be seen gave the architect a completely free hand, or indeed, the suggestion is that originality was an actual requirement. For example, the outline of the entrances to the Villa Stein (see fig. 33), with its lines oscillating between calculated geometry and dynamic tension makes this something that had not previously existed in the history of architecture – and whose genesis is central to our approach. Its curved shapes, which react in a sophisticated way to various circulation requirements, are linked by a diagonal wall which transfers the movement to the steps leading to the first floor. A three-dimensional backdrop is created here, carefully staged, responding to the point of view of the person coming in and derived from the simple motif of walls

50

Fig. 33
Fig. 34

The drive

• *Villa Stein/de Monzie, partial view of the entrance side*

[38] Details in Benton, "Les villas de Le Corbusier et Pierre Jeanneret 1920–1930", Paris 1984; English edition: "The Villas of Le Corbusier and Pierre Jeanneret 1920–1930", London 1987.
[39] Von Moos, "Le Corbusier", p. 135.

running freely within an orthogonal grid of supports in early designs.

Almost five years after the comparatively small Besnus House and designs that are important to Le Corbusier's development but outside the scope of this book, the principles of the Dom-ino, which had matured over a long period, are present to an almost excessive extent in this building. The wall no longer depends on primarily functional conditions. It flows freely, and detaches itself from all requirements to which a medium for forces and statics is exposed. In other words, spatial outlines no longer result from prescribed dimensions and necessities, but develop as a figure in their own right according to an independent design intention. The designer himself appears more powerfully on the scene, and the subjectivity of individual decisions is emphasized. This element of *design imbued by subjectivity* becomes an essential component of Le Corbuiser's architecture from now on: as Huse[40] describes, here the architect, rather than the external requirements, emerges to a particular extent as the creator of the necessity of the ground plan. The images, in other words the plan figures that emerge, do not arise from a prescribed set of needs, but are "invented" by the architect's structuring work. Thus function is derived from form – the opposite of what people like to see as functionalism, often in Le Corbusier's case as well.

The Villa Stein/de Monzie is a type of building in which Le Corbusier takes up the Citrohan principles, but reinterprets them. These are no longer variations on a slender building, almost like an inner-city infill plot, closed on its long sides and with a two-storey living-room. Here it is the short sides that have closed walls, with the long wall with their wide apertures seeming to be "stretched" between them. Two-storey zones are arranged on various levels, so that a diverse vertical penetration of the space results.

Four piers are an assertive presence after one has come into the entrance hall. They are oriented axially to the entrance, and establish a scale of their own in terms of the distance between them. It becomes clear from the ground plan that this dimension fixes the layout of the house as a whole, creating a changing rhythm. The piers define a kind of circulation track, once at the main en-

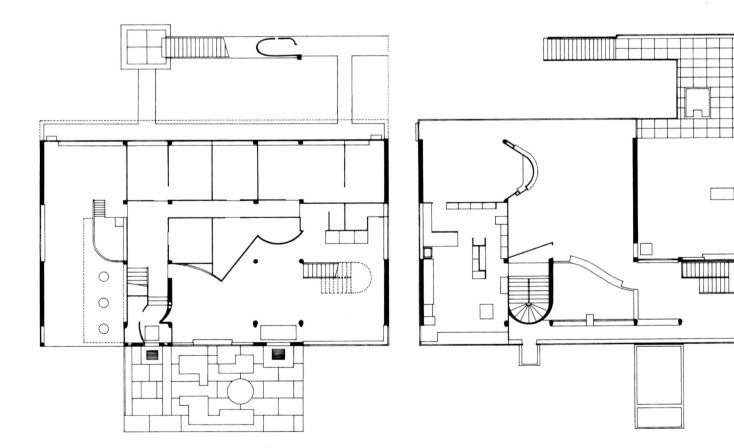

Fig. 33 Ground floor plan for the Villa Stein (redrawn after Le Corbusier by Klaus-Peter Gast, 1999)

Fig. 34 First floor plan for the Villa Stein (redrawn after Le Corbusier by Klaus-Peter Gast, 1999)

[40] Huse, "Le Corbusier", p. 26.

trance and then at the so-called servants' entrance on the left, features that also stand out in the entrance façade. Thus the ground plan is broken down into five zones, three broad and two narrow fields. The side rooms are placed on the grid pattern behind the hall, the garage is on the left, and an open staircase sculpture in the hall leads to the main living area upstairs (see fig. 34). There one is confronted with an extremely surprising spatial sequence: this is again, or indeed still, a kind of entrance, nowhere making it possible to gain a clear impression of the spatial connections lying ahead. On the left is a "non-space", a narrow promenade along the outer wall, which opens evenly along its horizontal length. On its inside this promenade is bounded by the piers of the supporting structure and a shelf sculpture, as a parapet to screen the drop to the hall below. A space without a function, it would appear, and yet this promenade does have an unambiguous "function": it is

Entrance side with servants' entrance on the left

a space *just for architecture itself*. It is a "transition zone" (Louis I. Kahn) between outside and inside, also an interface at which the magnificently enjoyable outside space is linked both with the changing inside of the same level and the hall beneath, a "promenade architecturale" in the purest sense. No other function obtrudes. An outlook point with balcony, placed at right angles, forms a clearly defined conclusion at the other end.

The allocation of functional areas within this ground plan is equally surprising (see ill. p. 57). In the intermediate area between two zones that are clearly bounded at right angles, a very generously endowed kitchen on the left and an outside terrace of extraordinarily large dimensions, boundaries "oscillate" almost freely. The two kitchen and terrace spaces, however contrasting their content might be, jointly represent "fixed" areas within the layout of the ground plan, between which the rest of the component figures "move". The oscillating elements, i.e. connecting or indeed dividing elements that move suggestively, function as guides along the way. A contrasting pair emerges, representing rigidity and movement, fixing and ceasing, in which the curved figures, like suspended ribbons, seem just to have detached themselves and the areas attached to them from the outside walls. On the rear of the building as well there is a free, narrow interior zone directly accompanying the façade. This leads to the observation that *the exterior walls are expanding*: the extension of the overall volume by the dimensions of the outer zones of space, which manifest themselves at the points where the windows are taken round the corners, is revealed as a show of strength mainly at the oval piers on the entrance side. The essentially tear-shaped outline of these extending round piers could have "frozen" the dynamic of this process. Three of the piers, linked together by a shelving system, "hang" on the curved parapet that is tensed like a spring by the suggestive outward pull. It could have been Le Corbusier's unspoken intention when developing this tension-charged ground plan to illustrate the *process* by which the outer wall detaches itself from the support system, the latent energy of which is still comprehensibly present.

A kind of "leftover space" between the right-angled figures of the kitchen and the terrace forms the actual living area. A second staircase – not necessarily for servants only – "sticks" to the kitchen wall. It is striking that the previously described ancillary-room zone made up of kitchen, terrace and access uses the greater part of the entire space, so that in terms of dimensions classical spatial hierarchy is practically turned upside down.

Le Corbusier's support structure is still clearly comprehensible on the ground floor, but it becomes completely blurred on the first floor. Only the piers, teardrop-shaped here, bordering and thus defining the transition zone, suggest the two structural zones on the ground floor, but they are only partly visible. The rearmost level of the piers, along the rear façade, also merges into walls, but their outer line remains intelligible. They establish the distance from the rear "transition zone", an area corresponding to the corridor in the entrance façade, which here too makes it possible to "wander"

Strip windows running round the corners on the entrance side

Strip windows running round the corners on the rear side, with protruding volume

Window detail on the entrance side

Entrance side

along the outer wall. What remains to be established is that this spatial track on the outer wall performs yet another "function", that of celebrating a continuous window following the whole of the outer wall. The long strip window, one of the sanctified principles of Le Corbusier's work at this time, actually needs an equivalent continuous space, which is now introduced at this point. It is hard to avoid the impression that Le Corbusier used a trick to harmonize the continuum of windows and space, which was possible only by detaching this continuum from the support system. However, the area that is actually allotted to the continuous windows, which is divided into two different zones, contrasts with the form of the horizontal continuous windows in both the rear and entrance façades, because it develops in *depth* and not in length. Thus form and function contradict each other in a certain sense. In his well-known essay with the questionably critical and ironic title "The Mathematics of the Ideal Villa", Rowe[41] addresses the rhythm of the support system and the consequent division of the ground plan into what Le Corbusier called the A-B-A-B-A (2 : 1 : 2 : 1 : 2) system, and compares it with Palladio's rhythms. It remains to be seen how much this comparison provides meaningful insights, but it is clear that the system for arranging the supports was used to establish the fundamental structure of the design for the Villa Stein that was finally realized (though

54

Garden side

Benton[42] lists numerous variants in which other concepts dominate). Here we will concentrate on the definitive design. Our examination of the genesis of the structure described using plan analysis is also centred on the support system. We have already mentioned that the support system creates axes that are reflected in the façades. The assertion that often occurs – as in Rowe – that historical references, indeed concrete models are revealed by symmetries and axes, for example, is certainly correct. But the hypothesis to be examined here is that it will not be possible to capture an all-embracing mind like that of Le Corbusier on the plane of interpretation of historical quotation and the world of phenomena. It is certain that he was able to draw on certain other criteria from a reservoir, a wide-ranging stock of ideas.

And indeed, one main element of the Villa Stein façades turns out to be quite unhistorical: the innovative, consistently horizontal layering. The complete denial of constructive, in other words vertical, structures in the image presented by the façade, and the renunciation of constructive order associated with this is utterly "modern", as it makes the façade into an almost autonomous part of the design that represents only itself. It becomes independent, and this assertive independence is celebrated by the horizontal strip window, if possible running the full length of the building, or even taken round corners, as in this building. The double strip windows with their dark frames in the main façade, which because of their special position are to be seen as two-dimensional, split the volume of the building into three horizontal strips. The bottom one is largely broken up by apertures, so that the dimensions and impression of mass are determined by the two light strips above, of unequal width. At this point it becomes clear why Le Corbusier needed these areas and especially the extremely high wall as an upper conclusion for the building: on the one hand they give the impression of two "heavy", oppressive volumes that *float freely* above each other, completely separate from the base, their constructive support, an impression that is almost contradictory, and puzzling. On the other hand they suggest that they are essentially thin-skinned, membrane-like, as the window and wall areas are completely flush with each other. In this way construction is denied on the one hand, but equally emphasized, as the novelty of the puzzling solution also means that innovative constructive methods are being exploited. As in the ground plan, opposed, contradictory elements are used in the façades, in order to create ambiguities in meaning. The balcony incised top centre at first inspires the perception of mass through depth, but soon the perception of stretched walls as partially dissolved membranes pre-

[41] Rowe, "The Mathematics of the Ideal Villa and Other Essays", pp. 1–17.

[42] Benton, "Les Villas de Le Corbusier ...", Villa Stein.

Garden facade with terrace area on the left

55

Garden side

Border of the plot at the garden side

vails. Weighing down and floating, solidity and dissolution, heaviness and lightness – exciting opposites are reconciled with each other. Riehl[43] asserts that in Le Corbusier's work and in the Villa Stein to a particular extent volume is largely created as "surrounding", in other words by clearly perceptible wall slabs. But the explanations above make it clear that in the reconciled contrasts of the design elements the volume here "wants" to be both wall and body. It is only the contrasting double meaning that produces the oscillating effect of a puzzle picture. Despite the frontal quality in the long approach to the building consciously stages as an *apparent* two-dimensionality, the perception of corporeal volumes remains intended.

Rowe and Slutzky's[44] analysis "Transparency" is still a model piece of work. They point out how much the internal spatial relationships of layers and wall planes has to be seen as dependent on the façades of this building. The significance of the external layer of space along

Garden side with rooftop structures ("ship's deck")

the façades in particular is taken as a basis for a more thorough examination of the way in which various levels that are stacked one behind the other overlap, not just horizontally, but vertically as well. The rear façade, which is more markedly broken up, together with the extremely deep external terrace may have been intended to make these complex layerings[45] visible on the outside. Unfortunately this idea is hampered by an essentially simple point in housing practice: because the sunlight was probably far too strong, the large area of glazing is never shown without curtains except in the photographs published by Le Corbusier himself. The suspicion remains that Le Corbusier possibly put in the strip window for its own sake in the first place, as a *formal* element. It will always remain a matter of per-

sonal judgement to decide how much the rythmic interruption of the wall by the strip window and the "even" lighting that this provides is beneficial to the residents, rather than alternating zones of light and shade.[46] The strip windows are intended to suggest the aesthetic of industrial, and thus cheap, production, in the same way as many details like banisters and fittings are based on this standard, concealing the fact that these features were expensively custom-made, and merely pretend to be mass-produced.

Thus the Villa Stein/de Monzie is full of contradictions in both its structure and appearance. It can be assumed that alongside the carefully calculated poles of rationality and irrationality in the design, with all its surprising elements, the formal language, especially in terms of the details, was intended to express contradictions, and thus to disturb. The expensive manufacture of apparently mass-produced goods also leads to the delicate and decadent spectacle of the rich upper-middle classes revelling in the "Arte Povera" of people who are less well off.

As Hilpert[47] points out, the plan and the elevation show the same dimensions and – even more importantly – the same geometrical structure. The most important ordering principles within the two ground plans will now be presented in the context of their genesis, to show that the structural design of the building evolved on the basis of a complex system. Here it is important for the understanding of the plan analysis and also of the architecture itself that the regulating lines ("tracés régulateurs"), as Le Corbusier himself called them, which are always quoted when talking about the Villa Stein, do not represent geometrical relations as such, but the way in which *areas* and their edges relate to each other. Connecting areas visually, in other words seeing edges together to form areas, was Le Corbusier's intention, and it is this that makes it possible to perceive proportional figures in plan and elevation.

[43] Martin Riehl, "Vers une architecture – Das moderne Bauprogramm des Le Corbusier", Munich 1992.
[44] Colin Rowe and Robert Slutzky, "Transparency", Perspecta 8, The Yale Architectural Journal, New Haven 1984; new edition with a commentary by Bernhard Hoesli and an introduction by Werner Oechslin, Basel, Boston, Berlin 1997.

[45] See Rowe and Slutzky, new edition, pp. 22–28.
[46] From today's point of view the strip window seems to have lost its appeal, particularly in aesthetic terms, because of violent abuse by Le Corbusier's hordes of imitators.
[47] Thilo Hilpert, "Le Corbusier. Atelier der Ideen", Hamburg 1987, p. 108.

Façade detail with terrace roof

Façade detail on the garden side

Inside rooms on the first floor

Fig. 35   The predefined outline of the building is determined by the area proportions of the Golden Section. To this end, the diagonal of half a square of a defined size – the latter constituting the short side of the figure as a whole – inscribes an arc of a circle to the "bottom line". The point of intersection there determines the position of the long side of the Golden Section rectangle. The starting figure for the ensuing composition has thus been established. The axis of the square and its inner line form important traces for the individual plan figures. The strongly broken diagonal links the corner points of the Golden Section rectangle. In the following – and as in previous examples – it is the symbol for additional figures on these proportions.

Fig. 36   The outline that has now been fixed acquires a vertical symmetrical axis. The initial square is then reflected over this axis, thus producing symmetrical zones within the overall area with the aid of its own axis and its inner line. The central area where the squares overlap represents the crucial field for the position of the support structure. Here the axis and outline of the initial square are in a double relationship to each other.

Fig. 35

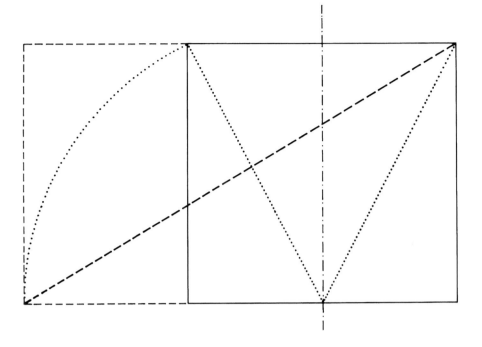

Fig. 36

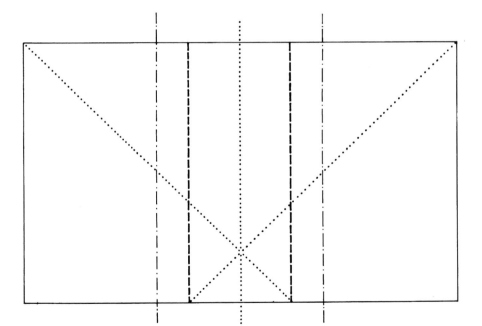

Fig. 35–40 Ground plan analysis of the Villa Stein

Fig. 37 The reflected axis of the initial square now forms two secondary axes. Each of them represent the middle of one of the entrance zones. The overlapping lines of the squares are reflected across these axes, thus establishing the narrow zones of the access area and of the columns. Following the geometrical logic, the outer zones of the overall outline – outside the square in each case – also form Golden Section areas (strong broken diagonals). Thus the rhythm of the layout is determined.

Fig. 38 The zones ensuing from the geometrical principle applied so far can be divided into the regular vertical strips A-B-A-B-A. Le Corbusier's designation of these zones is thus confirmed geometrically. The columns of a certain dimension are arranged within the narrow B strips, in a way that the outer lines of each of them lies on the trace. The distance between them was not chosen by way of squares, but develops from another relation: Golden Section diagonals starting on the upper side of the broad A strips producing a new horizontal trace. Around their horizontal middle axes they define the length of two distances between columns up to their outer traces. The length X, starting at the middle axis, can be repeated downwards, creating a narrow horizontal leftover zone C. Columns are also positioned on the outside of this.

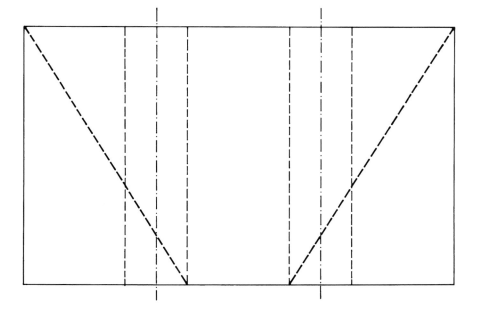

Fig. 37

61

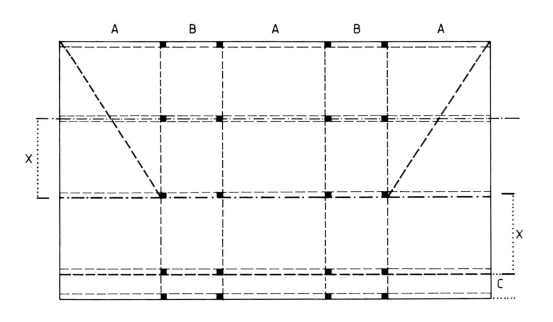

Fig. 38

Fig. 39
Walls of a defined size are added on the outside along the short sides. If now the Golden Section line – or also the "frame" – from figure 35 is shifted upwards by the distance C, this produces the same distance C on the upper long side. The line thus created represents the final outline of the building. The Golden Section frame "oscillates" by the distance C, or put in another way, the building *expands* upwards and downwards.

Here it is now completely clear that Le Corbusier is defining these outer space tracks as "dynamic" zones, distinctly articulated in the architecture as built by the strip windows running round the corners and also by distance from the wall and pier elements in the interior (see figs. 33 and 34). This also makes it possible to understand the teardrop piers on the entrance side, as the "process of distortion" of the outer line of the building that was asserted previously and is now made obvious by the geometrical system is echoed in the dynamic shape of the piers.

The B zones become access areas with the main and side entrances. Dividing walls can now be placed along the columns, creating a rectangular hall area at a certain point. This arises from the point of intersection of a Golden Section diagonal with the left trace of the B zone, a process that can be seen as a reversal from fig. 38, in which the distance between the columns was defined. The horizontal trace of this intersection (broken and dotted line), along which the walls run, also becomes important for a square that meets the axis of one of the B zones there. Its diagonal fixes the spacing of an entrance platform and the canopy over the main entrance at the point of its intersection with the extended outer line at the bottom.

Fig. 40
All the structurally significant plan positions on the ground floor have now been defined. Another important ground plan figure develops from the analysis of the first floor. The same square that defined the entrance zones in the outer area can be brought in here to determine the outline of the extended exterior terrace at the back. It cuts the axis of the B zone on the line of the horizontal trace from step 38. If the outer line of the building is extended upwards, the border with the attached flight of steps can be determined geometrically. This places a staircase platform at the end exactly on the trace of the B zone. It becomes clear that the orthogonal figures on the first floor, the kitchen and the outside terrace (cf. fig. 34) are unambiguously defined respectively by the proportion of the Golden Section and by the square.

Like key figures for the mysterious geometrical reading of the plan, the Golden Section and the square are preset figures within the dynamic spatial structure of the living level. Symbolically encoded within them is the contrasting pair, irrationality and rationality, that constantly inform the work of Le Corbusier.

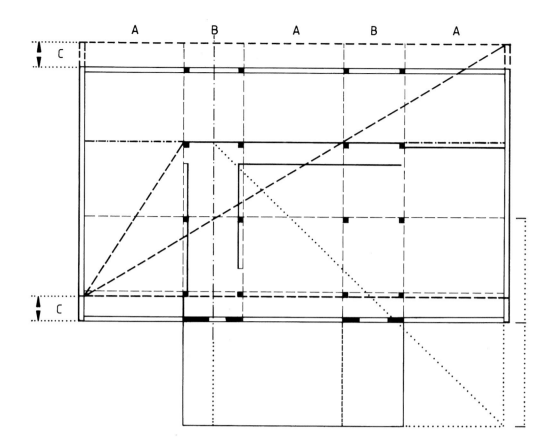

A   B   A   B   A

Fig. 39

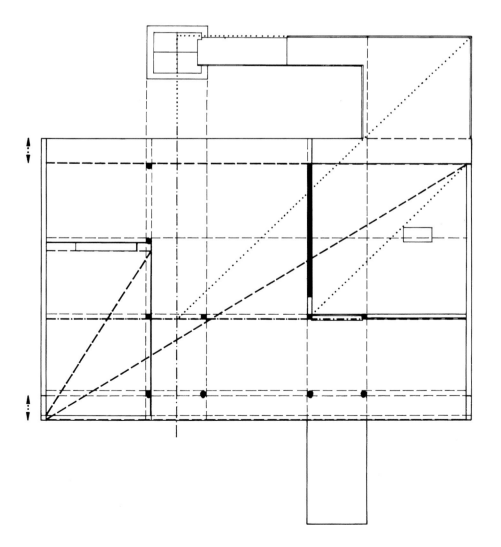

Fig. 40

Villa Savoye
1929–1931   Poissy near Paris   France

Le Corbusier's best-known and probably also most important building in the twenties sums up a theory that took concrete form over a period of more than 15 years, and was to have an enormous influence on emergent international Modernism. "Five Points of a New Architecture", written down around 1925, sum up this functional and aesthetic change. They became a formula for a new kind of building that was to be most directly expressed in the Villa Savoye – and it was also to be the last time this happened. More about that at the end of this account. And so a building emerged that was more a programme than an expression of the individual residents' needs. It would be quite right to assume that Le Corbusier in fact created a "need" by designing this house, making the most of this wonderful opportunity of being able to implement his thinking across the board, almost entirely without compromise. And the architect also had an international reputation by this time, which brought him a clientele that was very likely to want demonstrate the "avant-garde". This design is the glittering climax of Le Corbusier's first important phase, but it is also the end of it. It concludes his series of buildings dominated by the colour white and following a basic theoretical approach.

Fig. 41
Fig. 42
The house, originally placed on the periphery of an extensive, park-like, slightly sloping site, was intended as a second home outside busy Paris for the Savoye family. Here, more than in the Stein/de Monzie design, the car is built into the architecture as a symbol of progress. In fact it is the factor that makes it possible to live outside the city in this way. This "new" living means flexibility on the basis of mobility. Having a car means that one is no longer bound to a particular place, and people stay put only for a time, almost fleetingly. This state of affairs, a completely new approach to living and a new sense of vigour arising from mobility, has to be taken into account if this house is to be understood. "Movement" is a central concept within the structure of the design, which celebrates a "mobile character": on the ground floor there is a curve under the raised volume for the cars to drive on to directly, and they are parked diagonally, so that they are ready to drive off at any time. Diagonal walls suggest dynamics. But of course the curves also represent a welcome, contrasting figure with the angular, cuboid quality of the upper floor, as in the earlier designs, so that it remains unclear whether function led to form or vice versa. The dominant architectural

elements of the entrance hall are volumes for circulation: the famous ramp, symbolizing people who are spending time here, but on the move, and the upward spiral of the newel staircase as a dynamic element in the vertical dimension. A quartet of columns transforms the entrance into a space within a space, directing the movement towards the ramp in front of the visitor. Thus a person coming into the building experiences the ramp as a constantly present, determining element of symmetry, an axis around which the architecture develops in spatially different ways on either side. As the ramp can be seen at any time and almost from anywhere, the impression arises that a person spending time in this building is to be induced to keep moving all the time as well. Is Le Corbusier going to far here? Giedion's "Space-Time" element,[48] in which space and movement also include the dimension of time, seems entirely relevant to these contexts in the Villa Savoye. This absolutely

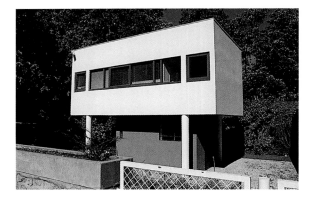

Gatehouse

open quality of the rooms on the first floor, the main living area, does not just provide a view, but also makes anyone living there extroverted. They expose themselves to the outside world, even though the immediate vicinity is not built up. This could give the impression that people are not "intended" to spend all too long in particular rooms, but to move around, and thus to "open up" the varied quality of the rooms and consequently the architecture itself. Perhaps Le Corbusier had been able to meet the owners' wishes in this way: Posener[49] asserts that they did nothing but throw parties there, which seems a little overdone. Be that as it may, the Savoyes did not live – or throw parties – in their famous house for very long, but this could be for different reasons, for example the fact that it was extremely badly built, and the rain came in everywhere. The lucidity of the ground floor (see fig. 41) contradicts the living floor (see fig. 42), which seems remarkably forced and complicated. Benton[50] found out that subsequent requests for change by the client led to this solution, and that greater lucidity had been intended.

[48] Sigfried Giedion, "Space, Time and Architecture", Cambridge, Mass. 1941.
[49] Julius Posener, Correspondence, in Riehl, "Vers une architecture …".
[50] Benton, "Les Villas de Le Corbusier …".

• *Villa Savoye, diagonal view from the south*

Drive side

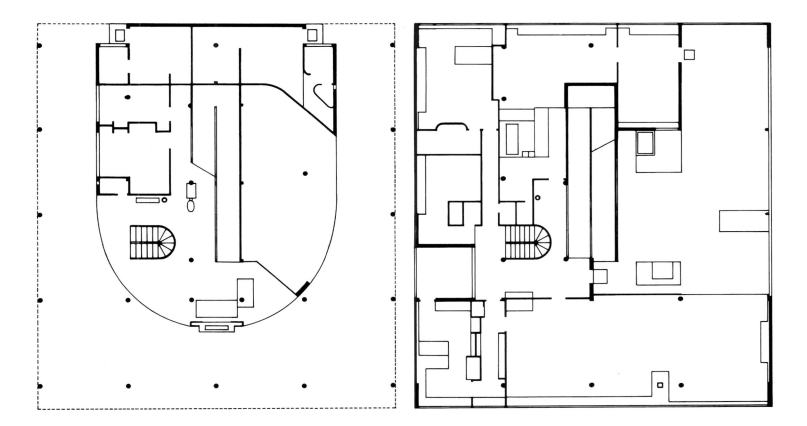

*Fig. 41 Ground floor plan of the Villa Savoye
(redrawn after Le Corbusier by Klaus-Peter Gast, 1999)*

*Fig. 42 First floor plan of the Villa Savoye
(redrawn after Le Corbusier by Klaus-Peter Gast, 1999)*

And yet Le Corbusier masters the complexity poetically. Difficult spots, like the corridor to the son's apartment, for example, are accentuated by a skylight and coloured wall designs, and its confined space presents a striking contrast with the spaciousness of other areas. The above-mentioned vertical quality in the circulation areas contrasts with the overall appearance of the building. The flat cuboid with strip windows on all sides expresses horizontality so succinctly that the vertical "counter-movement" seems almost indispensable. These two dimensions are placed in a tense, almost contradictory relationship with each other through an abundance of architectural means. The way in which the horizontal body of the upper floor seems to float on round columns is a powerful phenomenon, and it emphasizes the contrast with the round forms of the ground floor more than it suggests lightness. A large part of the apparently dematerialized ground floor area

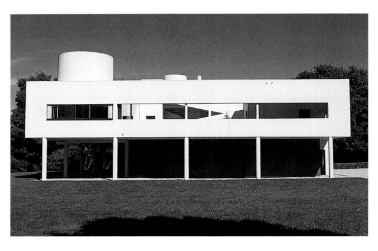

View from the south-west

is volume, even though it is glazed and makes use of colour, and therefore it constitutes a part of the volume as a whole with equal rights. The tangents of the round pilotis – themselves sculptures – on the two longer sides form the same plane as the cuboid of the upper floor – at least that is the intention – and thus they link it to the ground with their own line. On the road access side this relationship with the ground is clearly expressed. The volume that seems "raised on stilts" is in fact cantilevered, but Le Corbusier is playing with almost surreal effects of a seemingly load-bearing function. The cuboid is so heavily broken up by the full run of strip windows that the body of the building, which is actually heavy, seems transparent and light, as only wall slabs can actually be seen. In the same way the three-dimensional roof structures for the solarium form volumes as well as walls, according to the ob-

server's viewpoint, and are light and heavy at the same time. In a similar way to the Villa Stein, the dissolved strip windows make it possible to experience the layers of the interior, staggered one behind the other, from at least three sides, so that Rowe and Slutzky's complex concept of "transparency" is also applicable here. It is unmistakably possible to recognize from all angles that the curved structures on the roof are open, which means that the curved forms used in earlier designs are not given any further horizontal concluding level here, and so become self-confidently "independent". As well as this, they also include the sky as "space", thus establishing an emphatically vertical spatial orientation that also contradicts the breadth of the building as a whole. Expressive curvature, convex and concave in a most carefully calculated geometrical composition, contrasted with the prismatic overall forms in former design as well. The way in which these two configurations are combined here is new.

With the design of this building, Le Corbusier abandons the usual concept of orientation to two specific sides. All four façades of the dominant cuboid of the living level, which despite its detached quality is connected with the ground, are approximately the same. Despite a wide range of functions, the strip window is the only continuous aperture within the support zones that depict the ground plan square on the outside (in the terrace area it is present in the form of a slit without window-frame). *"Each element has an autonomous life,"* says Siza[51] and remarks that each component figure in the building proclaims itself independent. The façade here is even more autonomous than that of the Villa Stein/de Monzie. There is no longer any need of external "explanations" of what is going on inside, the communication level of the façade finally separates itself from the architectural content. The drama of the house, with or without extras, can be observed from the outside, voyeur-like, through the narrow, regular aperture. Even more strongly than at the Villa Stein/de Monzie the strip window remains an aperture for the sake of "form", showing the square inherent within the ground plan, that is "stretched" on two sides. This "stretching" is expressed on the extended sides by the greater distance of the strip window from the corner. It corresponds with the cuboid's projection beyond the columns. The dimension of this protrusion represents another "process of movement" on an abstract plane, which will be revealed in the geometrical analysis that follows. The building's geometry "oscillates", yet another formal analogy with the Villa Stein/de Monzie.

Why do we now have the regular strip window on all four sides? First of all, it is a formal dogma of Le Corbusier's, a formal invention that he boasts about and

[51] Alvaro Siza, in "In the Footsteps of Le Corbusier", New York 1991, various authors, p. 78.

Rooftop structures

whether the free plan and the free – and thus independent – façade were intended to create a new free – or liberated – human type. What was realized here for the Savoye family was their dream of a completely new, uninhibited life in an independent life situation, and thus the shade of a Utopia that it might be possible to build. But the aesthetic basis of the enterprise, "Five Points of a New Architecture", was not adequate for this task. It was not just this theory that foundered with the Villa Savoye, but also a view of the world brought up on the aesthetic dimension.

that demands to be used. But as well as this it is a "notch", an incision into the volume, evoking the above-mentioned contradiction, the double image, of heavy mass and light membrane at the same time. The upper, thicker strip of wall "exerts weight" and floats to the same extent. As it appears in the same form on all sides, thanks to the window, it seems three-dimensional on the diagonal, but slab-like in front view. It is only the strong effect of formal dissolution brought about by the slit, which mostly runs through to the end of the body of the building, that brings about this effect and makes the impression given oscillate. Of course it would be possible to argue functionally that it made sense for the building to be open in the same way on all four sides because of the natural surroundings. But this is not the main reason. The Villa Savoye is a model house, a piece of built theory, and ends the cycle of villa types open first on the short sides (Citrohan), then on the long sides (Stein/de Monzie) and now – the climax – on all four sides. The fact that the plot seems suited to this here is almost a side issue.

Studies bring a large number of formal analogies into play for this building: Hilpert[52] looks at the proportionally balanced ground floor and sees the face of the twenties tennis star Helen Wills, published by Ghyka in his analytical work on the Golden Section – which was well-known to Le Corbusier. Rowe[53] thinks that he can see references to Palladio's Villa Capra, called Rotonda, with its central dome, in the walls of the solarium as well as in the four evenly oriented sides – questionable connections made by a one-sided formal analogy. In contrast with this, Le Corbusier's statements on the "free plan" and the "free façade" are fundamental new definitions that admit direct historical references only with difficulty. Of course "memories" can have an important part to play, but they are memories from a stock so comprehensive that it is more like an unconscious store than a projector producing "models".

Finally the ideological dimension has to be addressed:

West view with drive-in and solarium rooftop structures

[52] Hilpert, "Atelier der Ideen", p. 91.
[53] Rowe, "The Mathematics of the Ideal Villa and other Essays", p. 13.

View from the east

Temporary condition with coloured paint on the solarium

Drive-in area with pilotis

Main entrance

1. The building on pilotis

Le Corbusier's demand that the building should be raised completely was never realized without compromise in any of his work. The pilotis became an aesthetic characteristic. Symbolic, like white, slender cylinders, they tended to be more like contrasting elements to the volume rather than an expression of constructive innovation. The space under the building that was supposedly gained usually degenerated into dark, draughty areas in which it was unpleasant to spend time.

2. The roof garden

The new flat roof construction system meant that the roof could be used as additional living space, giving an increased sense of well-being. But there was one factor that made it difficult to provide a satisfactory roof garden: in almost all cases poor construction led to a roof that was not waterproof, so that this idea also failed in the face of reality. But we should also point out Le Corbusier's desire for a "cosmic" connection for his architecture (which will be explained at a later stage).

3. The free plan

This was probably the most successful point, making a completely new relationship between the load-bearing system and the covering material possible. Le Corbusier created interior qualities that had been inconceivable hitherto. But what happened was that, unlike more conventional solutions, nothing had been gained in terms of the aesthetic principle in terms of this point, which is the one most directed at individual quality. The swarm of imitators usually reduced the new freedom to meagre dividing walls within a rigid grid system.

4. The strip window

The strip window on a uniform module extending the full length of the façade turned out to be of very limited use in practice. It turned out to be more of a formal element for developing charged contrasts and for producing a new sense of horizontal layering in the façade and seemed ideal for completely detaching the interior from the autonomous image presented by the façade. Misinterpretations by the next generation of architects also put paid to the aesthetic qualities of the strip window.

5. The free façade

Along with the free plan, the free, i. e. constructively independent, façade made it possible to break down the previous unity of plan and façade. There were now no conditions imposed, nor a sense that one was always dependent on the other. Le Corbusier underestimated the danger associated with this of leaving form and content entirely to their own devices as principal architectural dimensions that are dependent of each other, and to become independent and thus "formalistic".

The Villa Savoye is undoubtedly the purest embodiment of the Five Points that Le Corbusier tried to achieve. As this building was not followed by any other design working to this theoretical framework with absolute consistency, we may assume that to a certain extent it achieved the aim of setting up a programmatic manifesto and that also to a certain extent Le Corbusier sensed the restrictive and also unsatisfactory aspects of his requirements, so that he felt it necessary to change – or better to extend – the vocabulary.

As well as considering the formal-aesthetic and programmatic levels of the Villa Savoye, it remains to be asked what basic structural framework is concealed in the design. The following analysis of the ground and first floor plans is directed at the most important geometrical figures that determine the composition.

View of the upper floor from the ramp

Interior staircase

Partial view of stairs and ramp

View of the ramp from the entrance

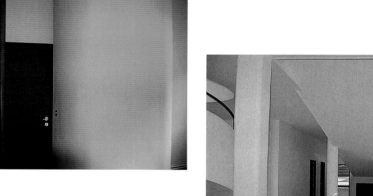

Entrance to the bedroom area

Bathroom

View from a bedroom

Kitchen

Fig. 43 A square of a defined size is the starting-point for the design. It provides a first proposition that is appropriate to the site, as it is not oriented.

Fig. 44 The square acquires a grid structure: dividing one side into four produces 16 individual squares and also a double axis. This is already an indication of "universal orientation", the approximate equal-sidedness of this design.

Fig. 45 The square is "stretched" on two opposite sides. A distance X is determined by connected area ratios in the proportions of the Golden Section (strong broken diagonals) with the "place of the right angle". Based on their respective points in the grid, on the available vertical axis, these right-angled triangles intersect with the extended outer line of the square and in this way determine X. The initial square "oscillates" in a vertical direction by the distance X.

Fig. 46 The short sides of this new "stretched" rectangle show the final line of the volume. On the two longer sides, it is now possible to add double squares intersecting on the horizontal axis, overlapping along the vertical axis. The overlap width on both sides of the axis forms the ramp as the central figure. A border-line of the ground floor volume emerges as the width of two central grid fields on the upper short side (the drive side).

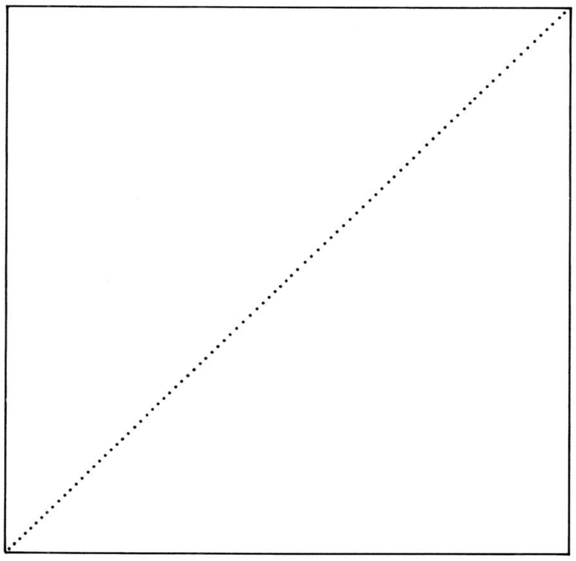

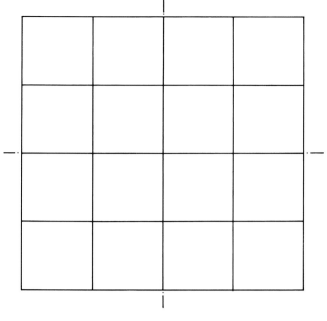

Fig. 43

Fig. 44

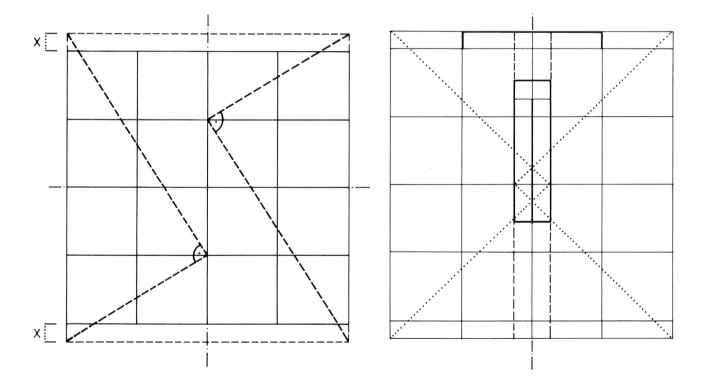

Fig. 45

Fig. 46

Fig. 43–50 Ground plan analysis of the Villa Savoye

Fig. 47 The grid provides the positions of the round columns as points of departure. Access figures are arranged between these columns. Here the proportional areas established in fig. 45 are important. Two Golden Section proportions, arranged symmetrically over the vertical axis, fix a grid point in terms of intersection point of the diagonals. A rectangular mark on the floor of the entrance is a manifestation of this procedure. The diagonals of the larger proportional figures now define the final positions for the ramp and the tangent of the curve of the stairs.

Fig. 48 A new area ratio determines the outlines of the ground floor zone. The proportion of 2 to 3 produces – simply counted off – two symmetrical areas that thus overlap (dotted and broken diagonals) in the lower half of the grid. They fix the border of the ground floor outline at the point where their diagonals intersect. This is where the main entrance is placed. The width of this area is fixed on a 2 to 3 ratio that causes diagonals from the point of intersection of both symmetrical axes to intersect with the upper original square figure. The radius of the established width determines the curve of the lower figure. It should be noted that the geometrical centre of the circle is somewhat below the grid trace, thus producing an additional powerful stretching of the semi-circle.

Establishing the definitive line of the central ramp implies that the central columns are turned into columns placed on the outline of the ramp. Here a regular spacing is selected that deviates from the grid and relates to the overall length. As the entrance is placed centrally as an extension of the ramp, there too the column set centrally on the axis is changed to two columns the same width as the ramp. The outer line of the columns on the long sides, their tangential point in each case, becomes the final outline of the building as a whole.

Thus the outline of the ground floor and the projected outline of the first floor are determined. The internal grid columns are omitted to make way for partition walls defining various functional areas like the garage. But the original grid remains present in the form of the columns in the outer space. It is possible to say that Le Corbusier started with the grid-like column arrangement, and then gradually liberated himself from it as the design proceeded. **Fig. 49**

A Golden Section area proportion (strong broken line) starting from the topmost column on the extreme right, determines the position of an entrance platform and the limits and form of the diagonal partition walls.

On the first floor Le Corbusier turns away almost completely from the remaining ground floor grid. Here partition walls form zones in which the columns either stand freely or are integrated. A very varied game is played with the independence of the two systems. The initial square is still unequivocally present in the wall slabs at the corners, the "oscillating width" of the square geometry. Its diagonal clearly defines corner positions for the various spaces down to the edges of the plant holders on the terrace. **Fig. 50**

The example of the Villa Savoye shows that in this built programmatic manifesto as well the geometrical calculation of the ground plans is driven by the square and the Golden Section proportion, in a state of mutual dependence. Starting with the proposition of the square as an initial figure, it is distorted by powerful oscillation. Thus rigidity and movement – as in the Villa Stein/de Monzie – make up a subtly dynamic pair of forces.

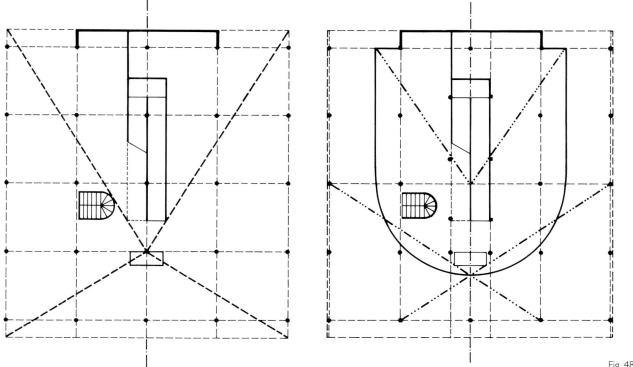

Fig. 47

Fig. 48

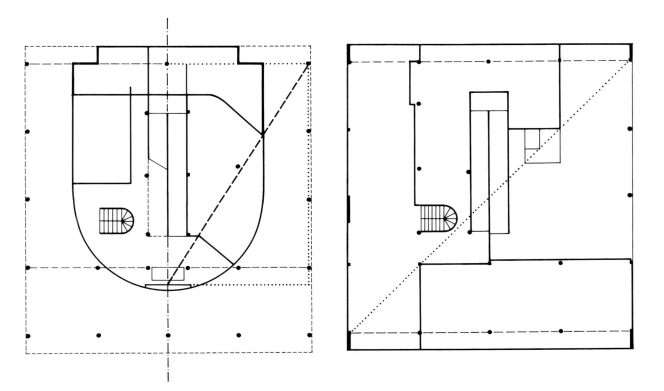

Fig. 49

Fig. 50

Ramp with solarium

Solarium

Ramp to solarium

Terrace

Terrace

Town Planning
1935/1946   Projects for Paris
and Saint-Dié   France

The transitional period between Le Corbusier's early work, which extends to the late twenties, and the later phase of his work is linked with the politically explosive period of European Fascism leading to the Second World War. This was when he produced his most important town planning work, as there was a lack of direct building commissions. Le Corbusier's interest in "urbanisme" – urban development or town planning – a concept that was not understood and acknowledged as a term until the work of Camillo Sitte, had in fact started to emerge even before his creative phase in Paris.

In the early years, when he was still finding his way, he was interested in various theories of urban design. So at first – following examples from Germany – he subscribed to medieval, less minutely planned structures, i.e. those that had grown amorphously, and then became enthusiastic about martial gestures by figures like Louis XIV or Haussmann. This spectrum suggests a receptive and growing awareness of the "town" as a structure, which until then had been largely incomprehensible, rather more than that he was developing or tending towards an independent theory on the matter. The persistent aspect as far as this subject is concerned is in fact Le Corbusier's passion. Regardless of critical social and political events he fights with unconcealed fervour for axes, huge scale and dimensions, anything that is magnificent, gargantuan, thus "monumental", and not only in the positive sense.

Thus the concept of the town acquires almost autonomous character as something that is complete in itself and independent of social relevance. "Town" becomes an idea that one-sidedly detaches itself from a complex context to become a separate "design object". It is not urban quality in a comprehensive sense that is increasingly to the fore in Le Corbusier's thinking, but *urban form* – handling a structure that needs to be planned as a whole and is thus defined as a *unit* with fixed boundaries.

Fig. 51
Fig. 52 This concept became an energy-charged design as early as 1922, with the "Contemporary City". Le Corbusier certainly does analyse the problems of given urban situations precisely and reaches apposite conclusions, though they have far-reaching consequences, but nevertheless his approach route to the problem of the city leads via form. Formal thinking dictates the plan and thus the predefined functional connections. The general plan for "City with Three Million Inhabitants" (see fig. 51) for his 'contemporary city' is an extremely disciplined *formal* design. The city is contained within a precisely tailored rectangle. Its prescribed grid and a square standing on its tip that stands out because of its diagonal axes are filled with key-pattern residential structures with "decorative" urban squares halfway along. Again following the original orthogonal figure, rectangular frames are defined at the centre that function as platforms and open spaces for cruciform high-rise buildings. Nothing can escape the diktat, sub-'*ordination*' is the key form in this concept, which excludes individuality and makes the inhabitants uni-'*form*'.

Figure 53 shows what a picturesque, almost idyllic idea Fig. 53 Le Corbusier actually had in mind. The relaxed view during afternoon tea from an enormous garden terrace of *uniform*, identically high and identically structured high-rise buildings in a green park landscape suggests enjoyment. But here the highly complex structure that is a "town" is reduced to a one-dimensional way of looking at things and forced into the template of homogenization. Never before had utopian town planners or town dreamers succeeded in realizing an entirely homogeneous urban mass that at the same time became a *sculpture* because of its uniformity. Le Corbusier is no exception to this, and we can assume that he was aware of the fact. Thus his persisting passion to produce things that could not be realized leads to the conclusion that the stirring, aggressive and provocative component was more important in his attempts to convey the visionary quality of his designs.

Gigantic and magnificent, sparkling and imbued with order, those were the words in which he described his high-rise prisms (see fig. 52), [54] which were intended to be built as a new commercial centre in central Paris in his "Plan Voisin" of 1935, in a similar way to those in his "Ville Contemporaine": urban form as a homogenized work of art, as a sculpture in geometrical excess. The 1935 residential key patterns in the "Ville Radieuse", in- Fig. 54 finitely long rows of buildings set first forward and then back, are contrasted with the cramped quality of large cities like Paris, New York and Buenos Aires as an example of less inhibited way of living. They are formalistic, large-scale shapes, and now they seem almost naïve, one-dimensional and ignoring human scale. Living, working and circulation become independent concepts and thus independent zones. "Circulation" is central to its inhabitants, who are constantly on the move, and symbolizes the mobility of the new nomad (in a similar way to the Villa Savoye). Thus urban form is also valid as the structure of the vehicle, whose network and grid Le Corbusier likes to spin out in a most lavish fashion.

54 Le Corbusier, "Urbanisme", 1925.

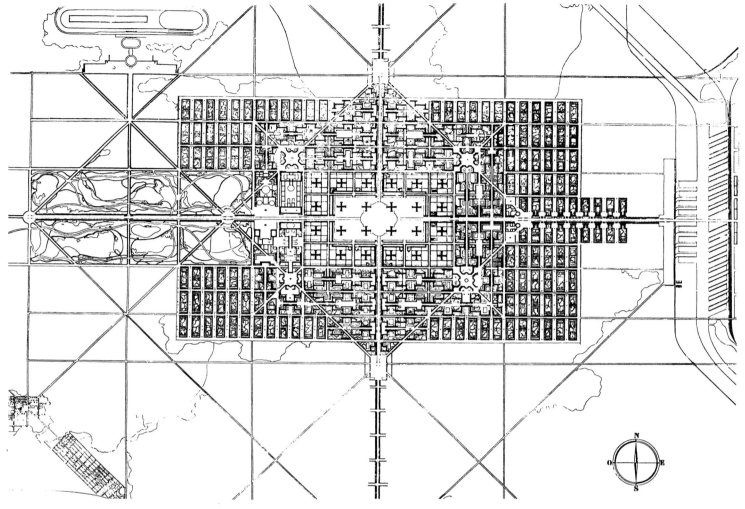

Fig. 51 "Plan for a City for Three Million Inhabitants", drawing by Le Corbusier

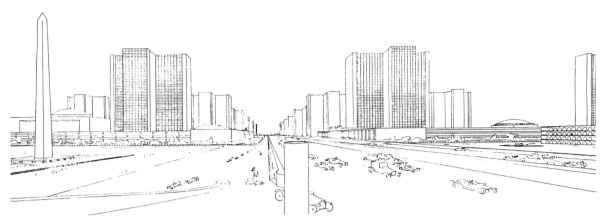

Fig. 52 *"Contemporary City for Three Million Inhabitants," drawing by Le Corbusier*

The *decomposition* of the city, already incorporated in the 1933 Charter of Athens, makes its pioneering debut here, which was to have far-reaching consequences.

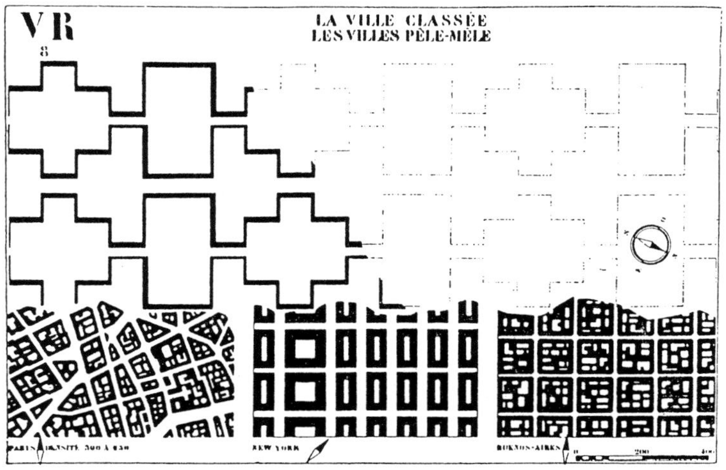

Fig. 54 *"The Radiant City," Le Corbusier's key pattern contrasts with traditional urban structures; drawing by Le Corbusier*

But the core of the statement sticks in the observer's mind because the ideas presented are so penetrating and impressive: new urban form must be *fundamentally* new. Here "order" and "ordering" are core images within aesthetically dramatized shock visions: the surprising impact made on the viewer is both programme and cool calculation. Here the ordering element of Le Corbusier's early designs for dwellings is transferred on to a scale that is beyond comprehension. Order no longer orders, it dominates. An almost eerie sense of constraint exudes from the urban designs that Le Corbusier intended to mean more freedom for the residents and more space and quality of home life for the individual. Creating order is itself revalued as an aesthetic and poetic process. Le Corbusier's language in his descriptions of this borders on polemic. One begins to wonder where does the ordering scale reach its limit: to what extent does the ordering thought retain its validity as a rational component? Where does the work of art end, where does the town begin? In his urban grouping of detached and terraced houses in Pessac near Bordeaux in 1925, which is being restored to its original condition in part at the time of writing, ordering principles from the individual buildings are transferred to the overall structure in a convincing fashion. The scale can still be perceived. But this structure is really a "housing estate".

Fig. 55

Le Corbusier's intention to create a city as a complete entity at one go fits in with planners' notions about so-called 'ideal cities' in past centuries. Like them, he treated structure as form. A megastructure is developed in terms of aesthetic categories and can use them to perform functions. New functional requirements, like for example motorways for handling mass transport, were welcome reasons for Le Corbusier for putting these categories into practice. This aestheticization conceals the real problem. Taking up certain principles of this thinking, but failing to recognize the "poetic" element of

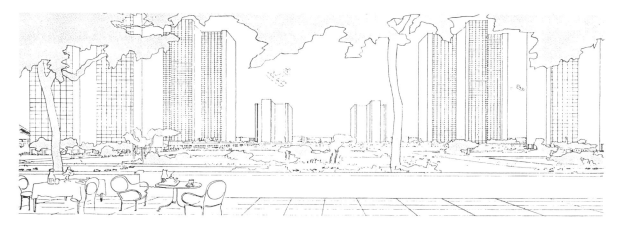

Fig. 53 *City for 3 million inhabitants, drawing by Le Corbusier*

Le Corbusier's planning and further reducing his view, restricted in this way, of the problems of the city led – and probably still does lead – to some catastrophic urban figurations all over the world. The problem with visionary designs, not just for an architect like Le Corbusier, but also for his contemporaries like Hilberseimer, van Esteren and Oud, was not fully grasped until later. In terms of consistency at least, Le Corbusier, like his predecessors, is subject to the fundamental intellectual error of assuming that everything can be planned in exactly the same way, and he acts on this error consistently. His urban visions seem logical, clear and convincing. They are uncompromisingly monumental, which is metaphysically justified by the right angle as the *"product of the universe"* (Le Corbusier). The city as an integrated work of art remains a Utopia. The *whole* of a city can never be conceived in the head of a single person, and the formal idea associated with this can probably apply only to parts of this complex structure. The highly complex combination of infrastructure, living space and working areas can never be completely grasped in its entirety by planning. Organic elements, in other words those that have grown out of history, hybrid blends as images of processual change, "unplanned" human additions by the inhabitants themselves and conflicting and contrasting zones in a complex – non-homogeneous – society represent only a few aspects of living in a city that largely do not fall within rational categories and here – of course – are excluded. An urban structure with subtle nuances that have matured into lasting value is not considered, but on the contrary completely suppressed. Anything that is not planned is not wanted here.

This book does not intend to examine Le Corbusier's urban design theories in every detail. As already emphasized, the aspect of order is to the fore in these observations. The example of plans for rebuilding Saint-Dié, a small town on the edge of the Vosges that was

83

Fig. 55 *The Pessac estate*

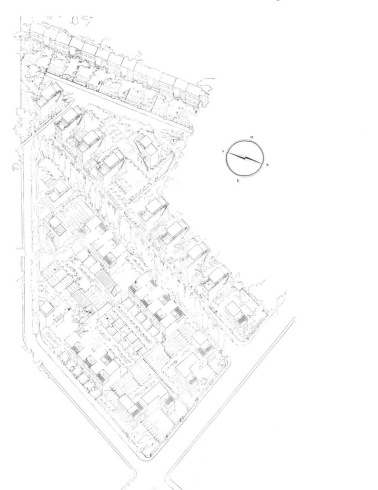

Fig. 56 Saint-Dié town centre, drawing by Le Corbusier

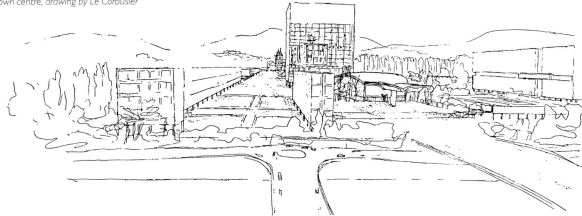

badly damaged in the war, may illustrate Le Corbusier's ideas in 1946 and shall be examined in their general characteristics and their logic geometrically and graphically. Here, in contrast with the large residential and commercial quarters in earlier plans, and the idea of

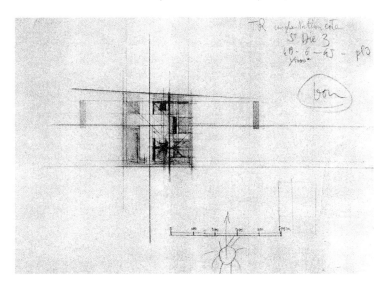

Fig. 57 First sketch of the Saint-Dié town centre, drawing by Le Corbusier

planning a town in a uniform and integrated way, Le Corbusier is more concerned to develop a new centre. Thus the medieval old town in Saint-Dié, which had largely been destroyed, was completely and uncompromisingly "cleared", but Le Corbusier did relate to existing topographical and structural links. Here the "old" becomes a background for his new, deliberately contrasting set-pieces: *"The old centres of Paris, Bogotá or Saint-Dié are nothing more than an attractive foil for the development of an urban show that obeys its own rules."*[55]

While the architect's early urban structures had to follow the "remorseless" geometrical laws of a preconceived structure, and buildings with different functions were woven in decoratively and formalistically, the de-

sign for the new centre of Saint-Dié creates *space* for the first time. It is not the structure, but the spatial context that is now crucial here, and the buildings, which do retain their independence as solitaires, are nevertheless related to each other in a meaningful fashion. Starting from a centre as an urban space with plateau-like lines and carefully placed solitaires, axes and the edges of building volumes create ordering links. The way in which the parts relate to each other can be shown by the following analytical sequence, which breaks down the geometrical dependencies.

In one of the first sketches for the project, which was not realized, it is possible to make out a framing square figure with two fundamental axial relationships. Individual figures emerge within the fields produced in this way, and they are clearly arranged on a basis of subordinated axes and diagonally related edges. This confirms Le Corbusier's intention of relating each part of the whole geometrically, to prevent it from falling apart and to make the composition seem uniform. Orthogonal figures, representing high-rise dwellings, are arranged along a horizontal axis outside the square, to create a spatial frame. This basic concept recurs in the final design.

Fig. 56

Fig. 57

55 Von Moos, "Le Corbusier", p. 160.

Fig. 58 Le Corbusier uses two existing churches to fix the field for the boundaries of a new development in Saint-Dié. In the north it is the outline of the cathedral and monastery that defines the development zone, and to the south, on the other side of the River Meurthe, another church outside the actual old town.

A square of a defined size is now placed by the cathedral with its axis on the towers on the west front.

Fig. 59 The chosen dimensions for the initial square becomes clear in the next figure. In it, the area proportion of the Golden Section develops geometrically from one half of the square and its projected diagonal. Obviously the distance between the façade of the cathedral and the axis of the church defines the long side of the Golden Section figure and consequently the dimension of the square.

This rectangle gives the primary field for the planning area, and from here it is possible to build up an ordering system relating to the solitaire buildings that have to be positioned.

Fig. 60 A zone can be established within the initial square established in fig. 58 whose lines create important links. It is a Golden Section area (strong broken diagonal) equivalent to the area outside the square to the south. Transferring it to the north-south orientation within the square produces an area whose left-hand edge (left-hand dotted line) establishes a circulation axis along the church façade across the river towards the cathedral. The point where this axis intersects with the horizontal axis of the square defines the location of the symmetrical and polygonal administrative high-rise building, the town hall. Its width is thus defined by the diagonal of the square. Reflecting the left borderline of the Golden Section area across the vertical axis of the square produces another circulation axis across the Meurthe to the right.

Fig. 58–65 Analysis of the urban structure of Saint-Dié

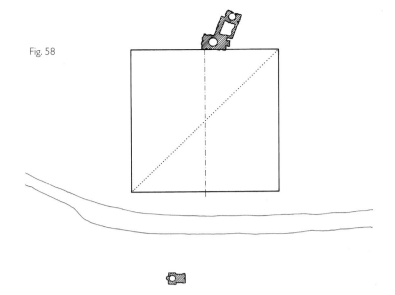

Fig. 58

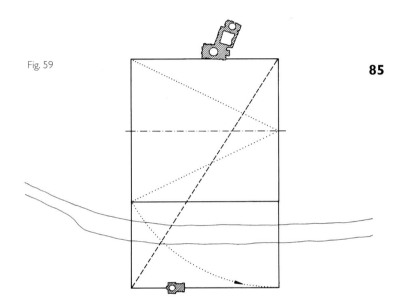

Fig. 59

85

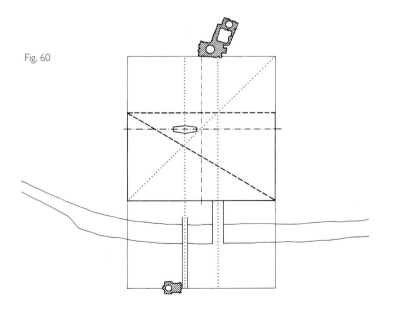

Fig. 60

Fig. 61   The new circulation axis – right-hand vertical, broken line – forms a new Golden Section area at the intersection point with the line A-A, the upper edge of the Golden Section figure of Fig. 60 (bold broken framing line). Dividing this into interdependent squares and the *minores* associated with this – smaller area figures – of the respective Golden Sections produces first of all another horizontal axis Z and also another intersection point with the line A-A. This point establishes a distance from the vertical axis of the initial square which is equivalent to the half of a new square set on the lower line of the initial square. The new square defines the boundaries of an inner, central urban square.

Fig. 62   Building lines pick up the geometrical lines of the new square. They confirm the existence of this new "frame" within the real design process, within which more geometrical links are constructed. The spiral figure of the museum is placed precisely on the diagonal that even seems to define the small side of the town hall at the intersection point with the left-hand vertical axis. A hotel follows the square frame top right. There it is possible to fix a square diagonal at the intersection point with the line A-A, which at its intersection point with the line of the square below defines the outer line of a long building for shops. The building's right-hand border on the urban square side is formed by the middle axis of the distance from the left line of the geometrical square to the axis of the town hall. Factory buildings are arranged along the downward extensions of the square sides across the river. The horizontal axis Z acquires its significance in the next step.

Fig. 63   Essential lines are thus settled. The shop building bottom left becomes an L-shaped figure whose left-hand edge is reminiscent of the square frame that dissolves there. The present step establishes other Golden Section proportions that are also important for the formation of building and urban lines. The Golden Section figure from figure 60 (strong broken diagonal from bottom left to top right) "oscillates" powerfully by a certain distance and thus fixes a line for a department store top left. This distance is also shown in the axis of the town hall in the form of free-standing walls or plinths for sculptures. The corner position of the department store forms another Golden Section proportion – immediately perceptible this time – with the corner of the museum.

The line of the museum now makes it possible to define a new line parallel to Z, a circulation axis extending beyond the borders of the area on both sides.

Fig. 64   The initial figure of the Golden Section frame between the cathedral and the church can now be extended to a square to determine the western limit of industrial facilities planned to be placed on the south side of the Meurthe. The proposed buildings' outer lines follow the trace of the square in a linear figure with intermediate yards. It is only now that the dimensions of two symmetrically arranged residential blocks can be fixed on the edge of the initial square. The diagonal of the new full square meets the lower trace of the circulation axis running out on both sides and thus determines the length and width of the buidings' rectangle precisely. These buildings were planned as high-rise accommodation like the Unité d'habitation realized shortly afterwards in Marseilles. They form the actual spatial border of the whole central area and define its dimensions. The line of the residential blocks now produces another square figure that fixes the upper border of the department store and the hotel. The two circulation axes running north-south are sight lines controlling the views of both the town hall tower and the cathedral.

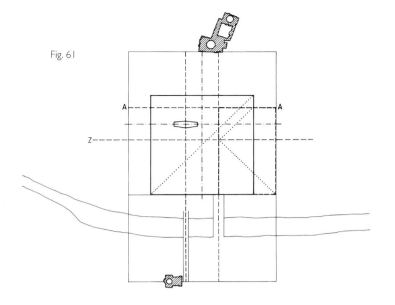

Fig. 61

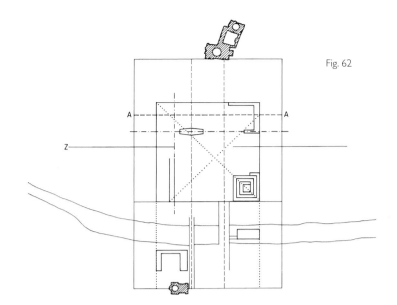

Fig. 62

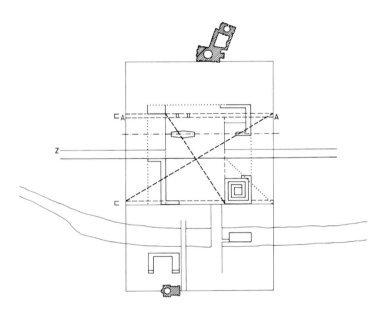

Fig. 63

87

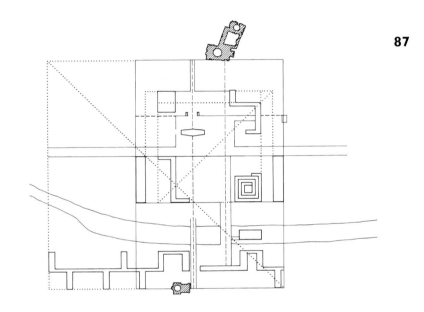

Fig. 64

Fig. 65 The finishing touches are put to the complex as a whole by two buildings on the axis of the initial square, which now clearly finds its framework in the residential blocks, the museum and the cathedral. These are buildings with public functions, zoning the two north-south links and dividing the area as a whole into two main urban squares. The left-hand axis is intended for cars, which turn off before the actual square, and the right-hand one for pedestrians. Le Corbusier's idea was that it should be possible to extend the band-like pattern of the factories, in other words the industrial zone, eastwards, without prescribing a concrete border.

The axiality of the design is emphasized and at the same time cancelled out by the interruption of the axes through clearly formulated borders formed by buildings. The axis is used here to combine different spatial sequences – extensions, constrictions, openings in four directions – by means of its imaginary trace. Thus *spatial strata* are linked up with each other. Hoesli describes it like this: *"In the ideal plan for Saint-Dié, the arrangement of layers is parallel to the Meurthe Valley; from the cross view it can be seen that the silhouette of the Vosges landscape has been incorporated into the architectural order, transformed into the ‚rear plane', and that ‚frontally displayed objects' have been clearly presented ‚in a shallow, abstracted space'. … In the idealized space of the layers, the long sides of the Unité assert the depth of real space."*[56]

Thus according to Rowe/Slutzky the spatial sequences moving diagonally and longitudinally are allocated ambiguously. They are spatially complex, to be related in different ways according to the observer's point of view, and thus fit in with Rowe and Slutzky's concept of *"transparency in the figurative sense"*. This character of the disposition of partial figures in the central area of Saint-Dié is crucial to the process of building up the ordering structure. Solitaires are related to each other – composed – in such a way that they follow a common order *unambiguously*, and create overall unity – despite the individuality of the different figures. But at the same time the solitaires have to be arranged within the ordering structure in such a way that *ambiguous* spatial sequences can be established.

[56] Bernhard Hoesli, in Rowe and Slutzky, "Transparency", new edition, commentary p. 62.

The example of the Saint-Dié project shows Le Corbusier's complex thinking and designing in relation to geometrical and proportional connections particularly clearly. He moves away from earlier rigid, formalistic concepts in favour of a composed ensemble that appears as a uniform whole despite its numerous parts. And yet in this context as well we should also point out the contradiction between appearance – solitaire buildings as an ordered whole – and a break-up in terms of content – zoning of functions. The division into dwellings (unités), work (industry on the other side of the river) and public activity in the centre (agora) destroys the idea of an integrated whole. Le Corbusier followed the idea of divided functions in town planning strictly to the end of his life. It must have struck him as a fundamental novelty, but it must also have convinced him. Creating something new that had not been there before has been in the foreground since 1922, and shows Le Corbusier's point of view. As Koolhaas commented on the subject: *"Le Corbusier's task is clear: before he can deliver the city with which he is pregnant, he has to prove that it does not yet exist."*[57]

Fig. 65 Town pattern of Saint-Dié
(redrawn after Le Corbusier by Klaus-Peter Gast, 1999)

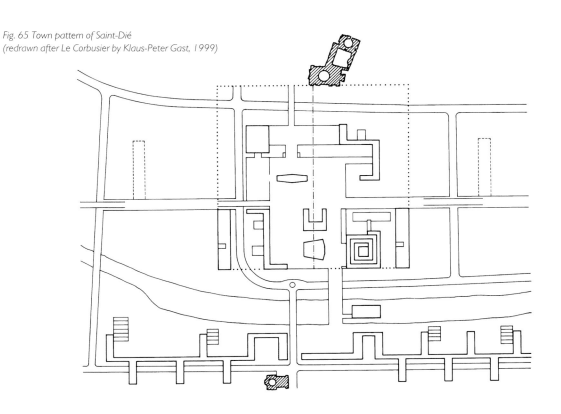

[57] Rem Koolhaas, in "In the Footsteps of Le Corbusier", New York 1991, various authors, p. 166.

Modulor
1942–1950

As well as his copious reflections on urban planning in the difficult period of the Second World War, when there were no commissions, Le Corbusier, far away from his abandoned Paris office, concerned himself intensively with questions of proportion. His passion about this subject led him to carry comprehensive studies that he also continued after the war and the occupation of Paris were over and he had gone back to his old office.

In 1950 Le Corbusier surprised the architectural world with a publication[58] that addressed the old subject of proportion, which had almost been forgotten by this time. In a very personal treatise, which he had been working on very carefully since 1942, he set up his own design *system* using proportional connections. For this he went back to his own designs, but particularly to examples from his life in general, to which he fixed his ideas that had developed into independent theses in the course of time. The selection of examples he presents is not ordered, in chronological order or even complete, but presents a random number of cases intended to illustrate, but also to "prove" his assertions. Le Corbusier cites historical buildings and their details, in order to test their *dimensions* against the dimensions he had developed within his own system, and find them confirmed. His assertions relate to proportions, for example the ratio of an aperture's, a section of a building's or a whole façade's width to its height. The subject of proportion had concerned Le Corbusier from his earliest plans, as his training was largely governed by proportions derived from nature.[59]

Something that had originally been a system of natural facts and that Le Corbusier, still working as Charles-Edouard Jeanneret at the time, had implemented in the earliest buildings he realized in La Chaux-de-Fonds as part of his decorative scheme, was later fixed within the approach of anthropocentric thinking, which became increasingly aware of the human being as a source of dimension and scale. But Le Corbusier established that the world of measured man was divided into two camps: metric scale, which he was familiar with and the world of feet and inches: the first an abstract measurement relating to the incomprehensible circumference of the earth, but simple to handle, and the second one derived directly from the human body (e. g. foot equals the length of a man's foot at 12 inches or 30.48 cm), but with the disadvantage of comparatively difficult arith-

metical operations. This led to efforts and an ambitious plan of finding a way that would bring the two measurement systems together, indeed finally make them redundant. To this end a ratio was called upon that was extraordinarily, if not outstandingly important for Le Corbusier: the Golden Section. As we have shown in this context ever since the Villa Schwob,[60] the Golden Section was central to all Le Corbusier's work. Linked with this is his unconditional faith in an *objective system of order* in nature, in the world, indeed in the whole universe, in which the Golden Section has a scientifically allotted role to play in as the ratio of parts, which is now to be applied to man's world of subjective design. Le Corbusier strikingly cites examples from all cultures in which – independently of each other – great art has been created with the assistance of the Golden Section. The "universal", timelessly valid aspect of this proportion leads as a base to a system of relations derived from it. Le Corbusier uses the concepts "modul(e)" and "nombre d'or" (the golden number) to produce a title for his publication, "Modulor". His book was acclaimed all over the world and the system of proportional measurements he described was widely recognized.

Belief in proportion and the associated geometry in architecture is directed at numbers and their combination. The phenomenon seems to be a purely mathematical one, but in architectural history it was usually visionary and romantic people who were moved by it. The rationale of design that can be precisely fixed in numbers is thus revealed as the key to something irrational, as proportion and geometry are not the work of man. Their existence means that they are merely to be "discovered", so that they can be used as a tool. The human being – and so here the architect in particular – must make this thing that is invisible yet latently always present into something visible – and will meet a well-nigh infinite range of possibilities.

It is not so much mathematics, that is to say calculated, straightforward calculation or proof using numbers, that is the main source of fascination in terms of proportion and geometry, but the link between evident logic, vividly demonstrated formulaically in an equation or in diagrams, and the things that are grasped purely emotionally, and lie outside human understanding: the intersection point of physics and metaphysics, an energy-charged point of polar tension. It is possible that here we have a primal source of true creation, an interface between the rational and the irrational. And this was how the Golden Section became the defining "measurement of all things" for Le Corbusier, a point of contact with the ordering power of the universe. "Order", expressed in geometry and proportion, becomes the

---

[58] Le Corbusier, "Le Modulor", Paris 1950; later "Modulor 2", Paris 1955, English edition "Modulor 2", London 1958.
[59] For this see in particular Brooks, "Le Corbusier's Formative Years".

[60] For this see note on the Golden Section on p. 96/97.

divine principle. The emotional force of the thought explains the Golden Section and thus its system as an "absolute": *"Here, the Gods play"*[61] he cries euphorically to the reader at the end of his book, meaning that when using the Golden Section there is an inexplicable element in play that art perfects. *"Hesitations and even errors of design are resolved in advance"*[62] by the Modulor, it says in the shorter version of Le Corbusier's complete works. This observation suggests the suspicion that here something is to be put in the architect's hands that automatically helps him to succeed. But this was a long way off the mark – the next generation's designs showed that a great deal that was simply mediocre was created by using the Modulor. Wittkower[63] firmly denies the instrumental character of the Modulor. Einstein's famous saying that the Modulor made it difficult to be bad and easy to be good is rejected. It is even asserted that it cannot balance subjective shortcomings and is thus more likely to lead to conflict.

The Golden Section is of course based on a belief in geometry and proportion that is thousands of years old but also, as a basis for Le Corbusier's thinking, on an anthropometric approach. The essential "classicism" of Le Corbusier's architecture lies in these two points. But this classical approach is now linked with aesthetic categories that were not there previously. The classical "rational" aspect of architecture, based on comprehensible ordering principles, here as always turns out to be usable in a new way and thus continues its life as a historical principle in Le Corbusier's work. Because he clings unyieldingly to these principles when designing, Le Corbusier's work can be seen as the most important element of continuity in 20th century architectural history; only Louis Kahn was to follow in his footsteps in the second half of the century.

Le Corbusier's most frequent application of the Golden Section naturally relates to the division ratio of a distance, but especially to an area ratio, as has already been shown in the previous examples of his work. The ratio of an area's breadth to its height is a defining factor in architectural design, and so Le Corbusier goes back to the Golden Section when developing his ground plans and elevations.

91

[61] Le Corbusier, "Le Modulor", p. 238.
[62] Willy Boesiger/Hans Girsberger (ed.), "Le Corbusier 1910–65", Zurich 1967, p. 292.
[63] Rudolf Wittkower, in "Four Great Makers of Modern Architecture", New York 1961, pp. 196–204.

The Golden Section proportion always requires a *square*, or, put in another way, it is the square that produces this very special proportion, as we shall see below. Le Corbusier's most frequent geometrical construction – both the simplest and the most obvious – divides the square into two halves. Working from the foot of the axis created, the diagonal of one half forms an arc of a circle that intersects with the extended side. This new side length relates to the starting length of the square in a ratio of 1.1618 to 1, thus establishing the proportion of the Golden Section. This newly acquired point can now be linked with an intersection point of the axis of the initial square. From there a line can be added at right angles that also meets an extended side of the square. In this way a new outline of a *double square* and its axis is generated geometrically from the simple initial square. In this way there are numerous relations with the Golden Section within the double square. Golden section relations can simply be fixed from what Le Corbusier calls the "place of the right angle" of the new double square. His "tracés régulateurs", for example often represent orthogonal arrangements of lines that show area ratios of this kind.

Fig. 66
Fig. 67
Fig. 68

92

Fig. 66

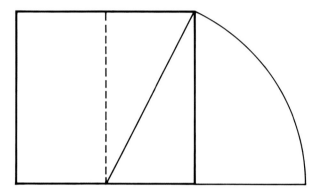

Fig. 67

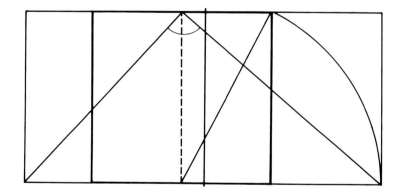

Fig. 68

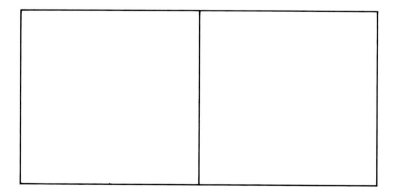

Fig. 66–68 Geometrical construction of
Golden Section ratios in a double square
(after Le Corbusier's Modulor)

Fig. 69   This basic figure of the double square, derived from a single square, forms the basis for all further considerations that Le Corbusier addressed in connection with his Modulor. This is where the anthropometric approach begins to make its presence felt. Le Corbusier relates the single square and the double square to the dimensions of a human being. The most important decision behind this approach is the guideline of a man who is six foot tall – 1.83 m – which Le Corbusier thought was the ideal height for a Western European, which is certainly something that critics could attack. Narrow hips, broad shoulders, long extremities and a small head make up an aestheticized ideal that seems to agree with the geometrical guidelines. The double square "contains" the man, it frames him: the navel is placed precisely at the centre point, in other words the axis, the slightly outstretched arm touches the upper edge and the fingertips of the hand stretching downwards touch the corner of the inner initial square. Given the guideline of the person 1.83 m/6 feet tall, defined measurements in the ration of the Golden Section are produced: height of the navel 1.13 m/3.7 feet, and of the downstretched hand at a height of 0.7 m/ 2.3 feet and the final measurement including the arm stretching upwards is 2.26 m/7.4 feet. Here it is crucial that the figures – and thus also the smaller ones derived from them – are derived from the single square on the one hand (right-hand column) and the double square on the other hand (left-hand column). Le Corbusier justifies these two columns of figures and their combination by relating them directly to the measurements of the chosen man and then uses them to determine all the dimensions of his buildings and furniture designs.

Of course we have to ask in how far women or for example Asiatic people, who tend to be smaller, were considered when establishing these figures and proportions. But this question never arises for Le Corbusier, even though the original Modulor man was only 1.75 m tall. The master also had an answer to this ready: *"I am … a poet: therefore dedicated to a search for the best, the purest of all things: and, in that search, the most*

Fig. 70   *intense of all searchers."*[64] English architecture students[65] provided an ironic answer to this inquiry. They hit the nail on the head, and Le Corbusier did not hesitate to publish this sketch.

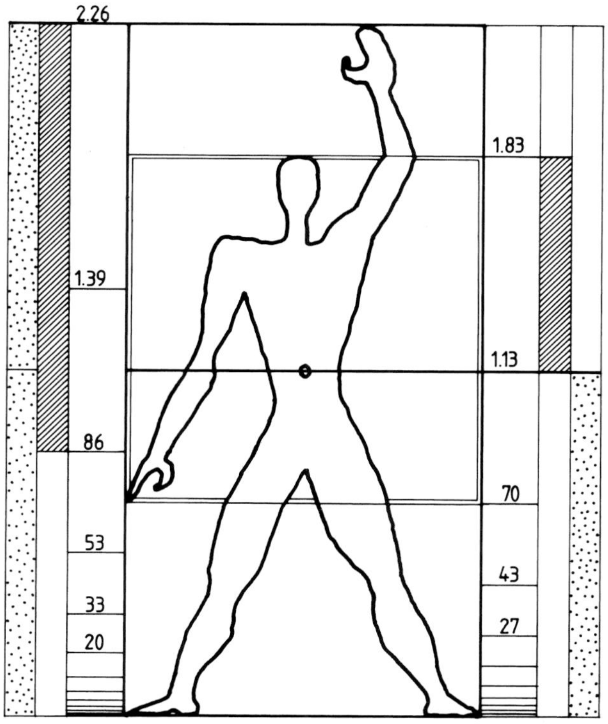

Fig. 69 "Modulor Man"
(redrawn after Le Corbusier by Klaus-Peter Gast, 1999)

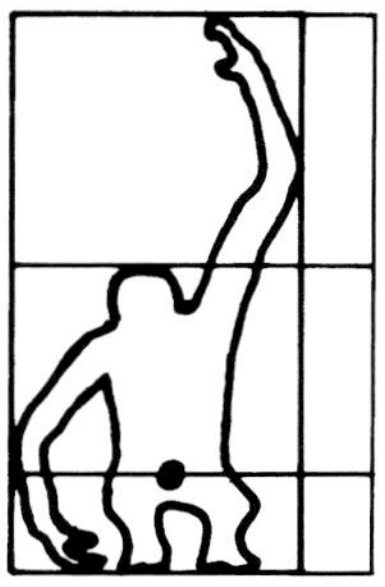

Fig. 70 Sketch by English architecture students on the subject of the Modulor (redrawn by Klaus-Peter Gast, 1999)

Fig. 71 Geometrical Golden Section construction
(redrawn after Le Corbusier by Klaus-Peter Gast, 1999)

93

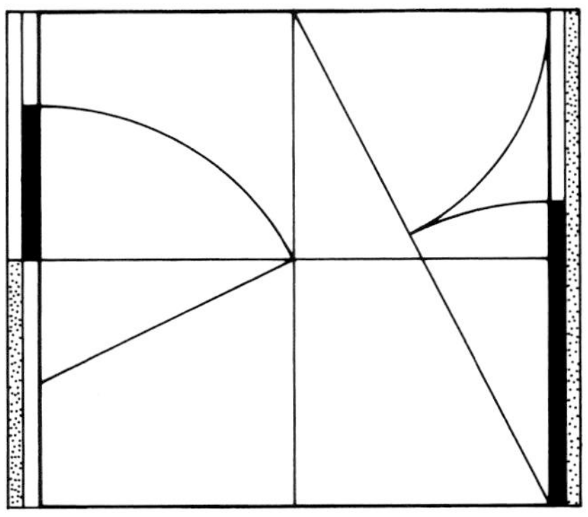

[64] Le Corbusier, "Modulor 2".
[65] Published in Le Corbusier, "Modulor 2", p. 24.

Le Corbusier's Modulor figures are restricted to ten to twelve derived from the single and the double square. He never tires of pointing out that his buildings were produced with these few figures – like a musical scale. But one must add that the conscious use of this combination of figures and their derivation did not start until the late forties, especially for the Unité d'habitation in Marseilles in 1947. His buildings before this do contain – as we have shown – Golden Section proportions and squares, but they are not yet "playing" Modulor.

Fig. 71 The fascinatingly close interlinking of square and Golden Section will be shown in the following in order to explore in detail Le Corbusier's boundless belief in, almost obsession with, the "truth" of these ratios. In the square shown here, two of the most important Golden Section constructions are juxtaposed, one in the left-hand half and one in the right-hand half. The left-hand method has already been demonstrated as the diagonal of half of an initial square, which reaches the Golden Section point via an arc of a circle. This is how the "major" of a starting figure or starting line is produced. In contrast with this, a double square (here in the right-hand half of the overall square) can be used to produce the Golden Section by projecting the radius of the circle of its shorter side on to its diagonal. From this point the Golden Section can be transferred by projecting the arc of the longer section of the diagonal on to the longer side of the double square. This establishes the "minor" of the starting figure.

The geometrical and graphical implementation of essentially abstract number values of course plays a crucial role within architectural design. It is not until a number ratio is "made visible" that the meaning and inner value of a proportion is established, so that the eye is in a position to grasp and control it. This also makes it clear why lines, in other words the outlines of a building or the borders of apertures, have to be related to other edges or lines in a façade or a ground plan. The eye identifies these connections, more or less consciously, and the viewer finally comes to a conclusion about these relations. It is a prerequisite for applying this approach that the architect actually intended to create "harmony" in the parts and the whole, as in the case of Le Corbusier. This kind of thinking and analysis cannot do justice to architectural approaches not based on rational principles.

Figure 72 shows a selection of the astonishing range of Golden Section relations that are possible within a square. After fixing a Golden Section proportion using one of the constructions described above, it is possible to develop or "discover" a large number of areas in the same proportion. All the diagonals shown here as independent graphic figures identify areas with the side ratios of the Golden Section. A kind of self-constructing principle seems to take over, so that associations with natural systems, those that grow biologically, seem justified. One particularly remarkable phenomenon in terms of Golden Section proportion, which further underlines what has just been said, is the converse fact that a theoretically infinite number of squares can be produced within a Golden Section area: a spiral figure of pure squares becoming smaller to infinity, produced as divisions of their "minor" Golden Section area in each case. Le Corbusier identifies the centres of these squares in his sketch, thus illustrating the Golden Section spiral. Giuseppe Terragni devotes his full attention to this geometrical figure in the thirties with his design for the so-called Danteum, a Dante museum in Rome, thus creating one of the twentieth century's great unbuilt architectural projects.

As the spiral is a dynamic figure, it seems reasonable to assume that the Golden Section is also a relation that emerged from a dynamic movement. In fact this has often been proved scientifically.[66] As the square is rigid and static in itself, cutting a line or dividing a surface on the Golden Section suggests the energy-releasing combination of rigidity on the one hand and dynamic movement on the other. Le Corbusier was aware of this pair of forces and likes to combine the power of the two principles. Something that is often expressed in his paintings and drawings is the fact that behind the boisterous, free and powerful lines there always lies an ordering, calming and restraining element. It emerges, as he explains in great detail himself,[67] as an *ordering network of lines*, and it is also there to introduce a kind of objective character into his subjective creations. This fighting pair of forces expresses a fundamental condition of Le Corbusier's soul, which often suggests that he is in fact fighting himself. Perhaps it is even mental anguish that causes untamed energy to be called into an "order". Or perhaps the will for order grows from Le Corbusier's longing for peace and balanced strength, qualities that were not granted to him throughout his life.

Fig. 72
Fig. 73
Fig. 74

[66] For this see also the note on the Golden Section on p. 96/97.
[67] Le Corbusier, "Le Modulor". Networks of lines within pictorial compositions.

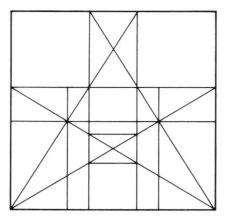

Fig. 72 Golden section proportions within a square

Fig. 73 The Golden Section rectangle with its spiral
of infinitely reducing squares

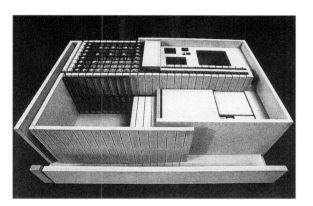

Model of the Danteum (design: G. Terragni)

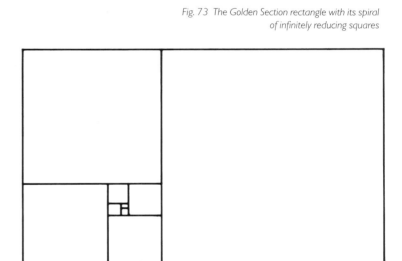

Fig. 74 Le Corbusier's sketch for the Golden Section rectangle

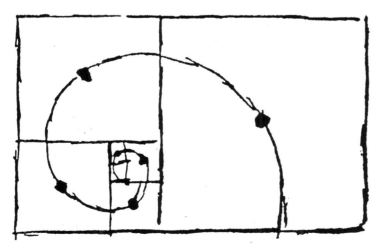

In the chronological sequence of the examples of Le Corbusier's work presented here, his advanced thinking about geometry and proportion took place during the Second World War and the immediate post-war period, and thus in the transitional phase from early to late work. Le Corbusier's experiences with applying rational principles to design are further processed and extended in the commissions that followed this pause for reflection. The Modulor becomes the all-embracing general principle for shaping all parts of the design. Rational principles are now applied to Le Corbusier's largest commission, that of planning the Indian city of Chandigarh, as he did for the unrealized urban development plan for Saint-Dié. Something that had so far been on a scale that could be grasped assumes almost inconceivable dimensions in a whole new town. And yet Le Corbusier unwaveringly follows his convictions about order, which seem to know no limitations of scale. The government quarter of Chandigarh, as discussed below, with all its prestigious buildings, shows how astonishingly Le Corbusier was able to lend weight to the *disposition* of the buildings by using his all-embracing Modulor principle, following a geometrical and proportional point of view.

NOTE ON GEOMETRICAL PRINCIPLES
The "Golden Section" was defined c. 1500 by Leonardo da Vinci as the "Sectia Aurea", and at the same time by the Italian theologian and mathematician Lucas de Burgo (1445–1514), also known as Paciolus, later called Luca Pacioli, in his writings as "La Divina Proportione" – presumed to have been taken from essays by his teacher Piero della Francesca –, it is also sometimes called "Divine Proportion" in English, and describes the irrational divisions of a line whose shorter part is in the same ratio to the longer one as that of the longer one to the whole; expressed as a formula:

$a : b = b : (a+b)$
expressed as a ratio of irrational numbers:
1 : 0.61803 or 1 : 1.61803

The simple geometrical construction of the Golden Section, preferred in this work, relates to the existence, always presumed, of the square whose half diagonal, transferred by circular arc construction to the side of the square, shows the line and area ratio of square to rectangle as the proportions of the Golden Section. Even at the beginning of the Egyptian high culture of the Old Empire in the Third Dynasty, about 2650 BC, we can see, in the first monumental structure in cut stone in the history of mankind, the "Step Mastaba", or step pyramid of King Djoser and his architect Imhotep in Sakkara an approximation of this construction in the ratio of diagonal ground plan length to height, and far more precisely in the ratio of breadth to height in the pyramid of Cheops in Giza in the subsequent period (detailed bibliography in: Sigfried Giedion, "Ewige Gegenwart", New York and Cologne 1965). The Golden Section was a division ratio known in Greek antiquity to Plato ("Timaeus") from Egypt, described by Euclid and Pythagoras, and in Rome by Vitruvius ("Ten Books on Architecture", preface to book 9), citing Plato and Pythagoras. This was later demonstrated by the medieval mathematician Leonardo da Pisa, known as Filius Bonacci, in a sequence of numbers formed by taking the sum of the two previous ones ("Fibonacci series", also known as the "Lamé series" after French mathematician Gabriel Lamé: 1, 2, 3, 5, 8, 13, 21, 34, 55, 89, 144, 233 etc.); as the size of the numbers increases, division of two adjacent ones provides a constantly growing approximation to the abstract value of the Golden Section. In the early Italian Renaissance "La Divina Proportione" can be seen in the structure of the Duomo in Florence (Saalman, London 1980). It was promoted particulary in the treatises of Alberti and Serlio and is said to have been behind pictorial compositions by Michelangelo (Linnenkamp, Graz 1980).

The Golden Section was the object of comprehensive scientific examinations in the 19th century. Adolf Zeising in particular ("Schriften zur Proportionslehre", Leipzig 1854–1888) and Franz Xaver Pfeifer ("Der Goldene Schnitt", Wiesbaden 1885) looked, like Plato, for evidence in the whole world system, which led to philosophical and metaphysical interpretations, seeing it as the apparent key to the structure of the universe: it is asserted that this proportion appears in the composition and structure of all living creatures, in the plant world, in the ratio of land to water on the terrestrial globe and finally in the relative planet constellations of the earth-solar system and the distances between arms of cosmic spiral nebulae.

Gustav Theodor Fechner ("Vorschule der Ästhetik", Leipzig 1878) and Pfeifer recognized the Golden Section as the result of a world "law" called the "principle of uniform linking of the multiple" ("natura diverso gaudet"). Multiplicity and "perfect constancy" (as a particular feature and distinction of the Golden Section as a division ratio) and the "mediation" of these constant division ratios can be illustrated mathematically in the simple addition of extreme ratios: $0:1$ plus $1:1$ gives $1:2$; $1:1$ plus $1:2$ gives $2:3$; $1:2$ plus $2:3$ gives $3:5$ etc. (Fibonacci series) and leads to the assertion: "The Golden Section is the expression of complete constancy and mediation". From this a natural-philosophical hypothesis can be derived: if the laws of constancy and mediation are to achieve full expression in nature, they would have to be expressed in the Golden Section. Fechner speaks of "man's need of multiplicity in active or receptive involvement ...", here in the sense of diversity and complexity, and allocates the proportions of the Golden Section pride of place in the human soul.

Dr. Anne Griswold Tyng, in "The Energy of Abstraction in Architecture: a Theory of Creativity", dissertation at the University of Pennsylvania, Philadelphia 1975, a long-standing colleague of Louis I. Kahn, addresses structural and repetitive systems in architecture as parallels to natural, biological systems. She discusses – here mentioned as examples – the occurence of the ratio $1:1.618$ as a distance within the structure of red blood corpuscles and $1:0.618$ as a reinforcement sequence within the brain in nerve synapses. Here she postulates that "Divine Proportion", the Golden Section, is the probable average value in the universe for repeatable procedures with two possible solutions.

Chandigarh General Plan
1951 India

The Second World War, that great physical and psychological break in this century, was also a break in Le Corbusier's life and work, but it did not definitely cut them in two. There were no commissions during the war, material adversity placed unwonted constraints on his usual way of life, and he was living in the south of France, far away from his abandoned Paris office. The break will also be visible within the chronological sequence of this account, which does not attempt a complete treatment of the œuvre, but confines itself to outstanding examples of the early and late work. After Le Corbusier's reflections on urban planning and the Modulor in this difficult transitional phase it becomes clear that subsequently his vocabulary is extended, but not fundamentally redefined. The analyses in this second section are intended to show that there is actually an evident, in other words comprehensible, continuity within his work as a whole. Le Corbusier started working again after the war with unremitting energy, especially in 1947 on the prototype for the Unité d'Habitation in Marseilles, which brought enormous difficulties with it, and finally in Chandigarh.

When Le Corbusier travelled to India in February 1951, the authorities responsible for planning the new capital of the North Indian state of Punjab already had a revised "master-plan" by the appointed architect that had been worked out by a predecessor. But they ought to have been able to imagine that this would not come about. Le Corbusier started again from the beginning.

URBAN STRUCTURE

Le Corbusier's office was contacted in summer 1950. This triggered intensive planning work that continued until he died in 1965. Le Corbusier's dream of a town planned it its entirety could now be realized at the foot of the Himalayas, after the loss of the old Punjabi capital, Lahore, to Pakistan.

The relevant facts about the framework for Chandigarh have been much published, and will be repeated here only briefly.

"City" is a long-term enterprise and can scarcely be planned or even judged within a man's lifetime. Thus Le Corbusier and his team of Western architects Jane Drew, Maxwell Fry and Pierre Jeanneret, working with a large number of Indian architects, planned the urban structure of Chandigarh as a "framework" that had to fill up independently in the course of time. The "bones"

Fig. 75

were prescribed, but the "flesh" had to grow of its own accord. The original plan was for a population of 150,000 and later of 500,000, but the attractive quality of the new kind of urban structure, the Indian population explosion and the division of the city into two led to the present 1.2 million inhabitants, if the proliferating environs are included. Le Corbusier himself designed the basic structure of the city with so-called sectors and the government quarter outside on the northern periphery. The other architects worked on filling in his structure. Each sector is about 800 × 1200 m in size, in other words a 400 m grid, and it is then divided into further "neighbourhoods", designed as coherent block structures or a collection of individual buildings. Each sector was to be an autonomous unit with independent supply facilities. A rigid grid for traffic, encompassing every sector, was intended to filter hierarchically the increased traffic anticipated by Le Corbusier, but reality has shown that everyone chooses the shortest link and takes no notice of theoretical guidelines. But it is clear that the traffic system works at least as far as the increased numbers of vehicles is concerned. Chandigarh is one of the few Indian cities in which daily movement is not hindered by kilometre-long jams, and so the amount of pollution produced remains considerably less than elsewhere. A "centre" – which only pedestrians are allowed to walk through – with public buildings and roughly in the middle of the town was also developed by Le Corbusier, but no dwellings were planned there. Other centres are the university and cultural facilities on the western periphery and an industrial area in the east. New shopping centres are now coming into being in the new sectors that have developed to the south, outside Le Corbusier's initial structure. Large green zones were to extend from north to south through the sectors in which there are schools and hospitals.

The structure of Chandigarh shows that Le Corbusier was realizing an idea that he had pursued throughout his life: the idea of dividing the functions of urban life. His aim of strictly separating housing, work, leisure and circulation was implemented here with all the problems that it entails, though not with the formal and aesthetic perfection of earlier planning. Both the anthropomorphic idea during planning – of the city as a human organism with head, body, heart, stomach and extremities – and the hierarchy of social life in classes are separating factors with far-reaching implications. Now, because the population has increased enormously and there has been subsequent work by Indian architects since Le Corbusier's death, the lucid concept has become increasingly blurred, which gives the city a heterogeneous and in this respect more clearly Indian

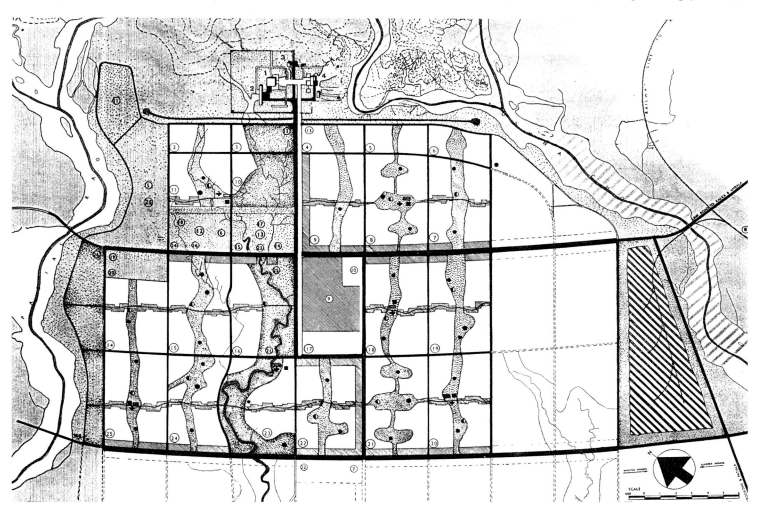

Fig. 75 Urban structure of Chandigarh, drawing by Le Corbusier

Capitol

1. Assembly Chamber
2. Secretariat
3. Governor's Palace
4. High Court

Public institutions of the City of Chandigarh

5. University
6. Stadium
7. General Market Reservation
8. Railway Station
9. Main Commercial Centre
10. Town Hall
11. Engineering College
12. Chief Minister's Residence
13. Chief Justice's Residence
14. Public Library
15. Museum

16. School of Arts and Crafts
17. Govt. College for Men
18. Govt. College for Women
19. Dental College and Hospital
20. Hospital
21. Maternity Hospital
22. Sarai
23. Theatre
24. Polytechnic Institute
25. Red Cross offices
26. Boy Scouts

character. Office forces had to be doubled after the state split into Punjab and Haryana. This meant an increased demand for public facilities and also for housing space, which developed into a permanently critical condition through political change and financial shortages. What Nehru, the first prime minister of an independent India, had seen as a prestigious political project and a symbol of a fresh start did in fact influence projects of this kind not just in India, but all over the world, though frequently not in a positive sense. Nehru said: "*(This city is) symbolic of the freedom of India, unfettered by the traditions of the past... an expression of the nation's faith in the future.*"**68**

Changing political situations over the years have required a flexibility in the urban structure that Le Corbusier's concept has stood up to very well. From the beginning the "skeleton framework" had been defined by the architects' language, who had been striving for homogeneity where heterogeneity was needed. The picture changed in the course of time, and diversity – in the height of the buildings as well – was introduced, partly at the price of more modest architectural quality. New urban figurations developed, like courtyard concepts and the concept of linked units and brought along the density that was required because in many instances the open development with small residential units and large green areas was at odds with the inhabitants' needs. In the seventies, increasing land speculation led to rising land prices, so that more residents had to be accommodated per unit. Also the "labour colonies" represented a significant problem: illegal accommodation built for themselves by the workers who were putting up official housing of all categories and swarming around the building sites. Even a government programme to create housing for the workers, who were intended to leave the city, failed through shortage

of money. So today the concrete buildings in the commercial centres mingle with the workers' mud huts.

Today Chandigarh with its block structures, street grid, predominantly uniform building heights and an established centre seems more like a conventional urban structure. Almost traditional, as all these components have been aspects of urban development considerations from time immemorial, and the separation of functions that was originally planned has been increasingly watered down. Here it has turned out in the course of time that Le Corbusier's rigorous and often criticized structure represents a stabilizing element in the continuing process of change within this urban experiment. It keeps the almost ulcerous proliferation that is peculiar to Indian towns in check and creates order in patterns that are otherwise organic and amorphous. Even Le Corbusier's astonishingly monotonous city centre with its attempt at imposing uniformity at any cost could turn out to be viable in future, as alterations by the users can be predicted that here will not damage the basic concept of an ordered whole because of the prescribed structure.

Thus it can be asserted that in developing Chandigarh Le Corbusier brought Utopian visions back to the plane on which they can be realized, so that ultimately he would have room for an urban structure that is driven by classical, tried-and-tested patterns. It is perhaps in this element, the linking of innovation and tradition, that the actual message of a task that is as complex as this lies. But there is one respect in which the urban concept is clearly different from traditional solutions of our times: in its relationship and position in terms of the government quarter. The so-called "Capitol" is symbolically at the head of the city, assuming that the north and the edge of the mountain range can be seen as an upper zone. There was never any suggestion that the

68 Quotation by Jawaharlal Nehru from: Peter Serenyi, "Timeless but of its Time, Le Corbusier's Architecture in India", Perspecta 20, The Yale Architectural Journal, Cambridge 1983, p. 163.

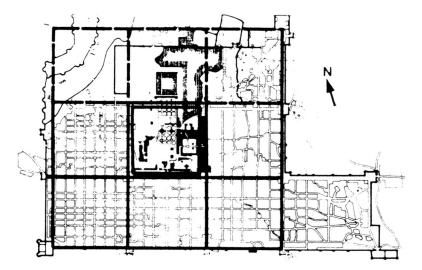

Fig. 76 The city of Jaipur (India) as a Mandala

urban area should be extended northwards to tie the government quarter into the urban structure, but development in the vicinity of the Capitol was expressly forbidden in the "Edict of Chandigarh", which was largely formulated by Le Corbusier. This isolation attracts attention and probably represents the most critical point in Le Corbusier's general plan. Its protected special position makes the government quarter into a special area, an untouchable zone, a sacred precinct, an Olympus.

THE CAPITOL COMPLEX

The city's main axes lead, like arteries, to the head of the urban development, the Capitol. Just as the government quarter is rhythmically filled with blood, the people who work there, so conversely it supplies the city's needs with its decisions, orders and legislation. "Circulation" conceived in this anthropomorphic way was the image on which this structure was based, and one that Le Corbusier sketched himself on many occasions. But it may be that memories of the Indian city of Jaipur played a part as well. Its square grids derived from the

Fig. 76

Mandala, a contemplative image, and a fortress outside present a very similar pattern. We shall mention only in passing that the isolation of the Capitol and the disposition of its buildings could also have evoked images of ancient models (Acropolis).

But this was certainly the first modern urban planning project to follow a concept of this kind so consistently. Why does Le Corbusier separate the government buildings from the city so dramatically? Of course the idea of prestige is at the top of his mind, and his demand for monumentality at all costs, which he would dearly like to express fully as an architect here. For he was very quickly clear about the fact that here he was dealing with clients who would not ask any supposedly

"unnecessary" questions and who had faith in the abilities and strength of the "inspired" architect from the West. Here is Balkrishna Doshi,[69] a former colleague from the Paris office, on criticism of the Capitol project:"*The people involved were overawed by the fact that he was a genius and also a foreigner and therefore thought that nothing could go wrong; they were hesitant to discuss functional issues with him. He didn't ask, they didn't question, so the blame lies with both parties. In any case Indians are generally too subservient to foreigners.*" This opportunity to build unhampered by objections – every architect's dream – was certainly welcome to Le Corbusier, after the contractual conditions had been sorted out and there seemed to be nothing else in the way of the job. But it is still reasonable to suspect that there must have been other and perhaps more important reasons for the special position of the complex than these psychological and strategic ones.

[69] Balkrishna Vithaldas Doshi, in architectura & natura quarterly (ANQ document): "Chandigarh, Forty Years After Le Corbusier", Amsterdam 1991, p. 28.

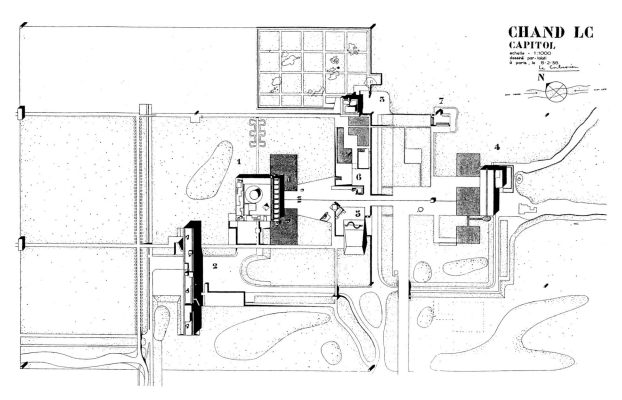

Fig. 77 General plan of the Chandigarh Capitol buildings, drawing by Le Corbusier

Fig. 77 In the original plan the Capitol consists of four individual buildings, the Parliament Building (1), the Secretariat (2), the High Court (4) and the Governor's Palace (3), which was ultimately not realized as a result of a personal objection from Nehru, as he felt that placing the Governor in such an eye-catching position was not compatible with the new democracy. Le Corbusier immediately suggested a Museum of Knowledge on the same site, but this was not built, even though the foundations were completed. Alongside these were some free-standing monuments, like the Open Hand (7) – eventually erected in 1985, with financial assistance from all over the world –, the monument for the victims of the partition of the state (6), the Tower of the Shadows, in the form of a pavilion with brise-soleil walls and an artificial mound of earth shaped like a truncated pyramid (5). The disposition of the buildings permits a surmise about Le Corbusier's intentions: here the parts are not only brought together as a composition that expresses the relations of the individual figures to each other and to the whole, but moreover the individual buildings remain in positions that are clearly isolated and almost *independent*. The latent geometry of this disposition is immediately perceptible, and underlined by platforms, site edges, the way in which paths relate and axes.

This all suggests that the elements were combined on the basis of a system. But the feature that Le Corbusier emphasized in the urban structure of Chandigarh, the

structural network as a unity, tying together, developing and becoming denser, is completely rejected here. "Density" is not something Le Corbusier is looking for in the Capitol, on the contrary, the enormous distance between the buildings is a quite astonishing element. This distance does not lead to an urban ensemble, intended to create "space" with its streets, squares, and wide and narrow parts. In fact the distance enables Le Corbusier to implement his intention of presenting each building for its own sake. *"Self"-representation* is the aim here, as Le Corbusier wants to rank each building as an independent sculpture, needing to stand freely as an individual. "Space" does not have a part to play here, but "expanse", the idea of presenting all this sculptural excess on a plateau. Even the Secretariat, which is basically just an office building, becomes an expressively powerful and thus monumental work of art in hands of Le Corbusier. The fact that they are so far apart makes it possible to look at each building without obstruction from many angles. From the central area of the complex, which is kept absolutely empty, and was intended as a "processional route" between the Parliament Building and the High Court, all the buildings present themselves completely openly to the observer. The usual interpretation is that the great distance between the Parliament Building and the High Court symbolizes the independence of legislature and executive. This is plausible, but certainly not Le Corbusier's main intention. For this reason the Capitol in

Secretariat

Secretariat and Parliament Building

Parliament Building and Tower of the Shadows

Capitol plaza

High Court right and Open Hand left

Chandigarh is not an urban forum, an active plaza where people could meet and communicate, as expressed in the design for the rebuilding of Saint-Dié (see fig. 65) in a way that was new at the time. Saint-Dié and the Capitol are often compared, but this is correct only in relation to the ordered, geometrically defined arrangement of solitaires that was first demonstrated impressively in Saint-Dié. There the edges of the buildings unambiguously create space, so that town centre activities can develop between the buildings. They also create space, or better multiply overlapping spaces to stimulate human activity against the backdrop of the Vosges mountains. Here in Chandigarh, the widely separated monuments are spread out against the lively background of the foothills of the Himalayas in such a way that it takes the mountains to establish a border for the space.

As we have seen, the disposition of the component figures in Saint-Dié is based on an inherent system of geometrical order. In the case of the Capitol, we assume that there is an ordering system, but this has still to be proved. Even a glance at Le Corbusier's plan (see fig. 77) shows that an ordering frame of this kind exists: a broad, square field, identified by tall, slender pillars, or steles (Le Corbusier calls them "obelisks"), marks off an area that corresponds with the width of one sector in the city. Le Corbusier's plan is now to transfer the system used to order the city, the 800 m sectors, to the government area, to introduce a unit of scale, the double 400 m grid. The plan suggests that the architect intended to extend the plan, as a road that is already drawn in and other access possibilities left of the Secretariat suggest that there might be more Capitol buildings to come. The large square field is the first regulator of the units of scale, complemented by two others, namely a double square on the horizontal axis of the large field containing the Capitol buildings themselves, also marked with steles. Le Corbusier tries to identify the planning borders of the Capitol for the future and to define clear limits for an extension. This makes it clear that both the grid measurement of 400 m with its sector dimension of 800 m and the associated system of proportional and geometrical order into which the Capitol buildings seem to be tied were an explicit part of the planning process. The fact that their fields are marked off with steles means that these dimensions were to remain a constant presence, unit of scale and *dimension*, and dependent on these, *proportion* are thus the crucial criteria for the disposition of the Capitol buildings, which reflect the inherent ordering system in their specific relation. One can only agree with Venezia's[70] observation that concealed behind the essentially two-dimensional placing of the buildings is a *rhythm* in the overall view from the south-west. The rhythm can be seen as proportional to the lines and axes, and thus indicates an inner order. This is the only way in which the apparently solitary Capitol buildings become a coherent whole, and it is not easy to understand this coherence when visiting the site. The "over-individualization" of the buildings because they are so far apart and the loss of a vividly unified whole withdraws almost completely from the human scale that Le Corbusier wanted to introduce here. This makes an impression that is all the more painful as important parts of the complex were never completed, and the huge expanse area between the Parliament Building and the High Court in particular has established itself as an empty, if not even a desolate field, almost waste land, which could not be further from the original plan. The fact that the composition is incomplete makes the distance seem even greater, and the "processional route" between the Parliament Building and the High Court looks all the more unattractive. The problems of the Capitol site emerge all the more clearly here: it is not just the isolation from a lively urban area that means that it is little used, or almost disregarded, but also the fact that any further development is forbidden. Other factors that have led to this slide into the condition of a steppe are a mentality of calm indifference, the disrespectful lack of maintenance and the extreme climate. And the "disfunctionality" (Doshi) inside the buildings also leads to difficulties, as needs specific to the region are not catered for.

Le Corbusier's structure for Chandigarh prescribed an urban framework that is in a position to develop dynamically. Here the ordering geometry takes a back seat to the independently proliferating mass of the city and a certain carefree way of life. The Capitol stands in marked contrast with this. Its rigid isolation means that it remains also in a kind of death-state. "Timeless" in Serenyi's sense[71] could here be seen as synonymous with "archaic". We sense associations with ancient sites: the Capitol as an archaeological find — a ruined city thousands of years old, rediscovered and excavated, with enormous empty spaces between the buildings, only occasionally populated with tourists. Lonely monuments with a strange black patina, representing only themselves and self-sufficient on a magic field — signs of a strange and distant world, but that somehow seems quite familiar to us. This is not the only contrast with the actual city, there is a formal and aesthetic one as well. The impressive, sculpted structures in the Capitol make extraordinarily high formal demands in comparison with the rather more modest city complex. Von Moos[72] goes so far as to suggest that the governmental buildings could be for a world government, and Fry

[70] Francesco Venezia, "On an Antique Frieze", in "In the Footsteps of Le Corbusier", New York 1991, various authors, pp. 209 ff.

[71] Serenyi, "Timeless but of its Time".
[72] Von Moos, "Le Corbusier", p. 309.

finds *"a justifiable element of exaggeration"*[73] in the Capitol area. It may be that Le Corbusier was following a secret intention of planning India's actual new capital, but this will remain for ever speculation.

Fig. 78   What we now have to do is reveal the crucial connections within the supposed inherent ordering structure that makes it possible to understand the disposition of the individual buildings. In one of the first sketches for the project, Le Corbusier drew a square for the city, divided by asymmetrically ordered axes. He added another square with another figure attached to it on the upper edge. This is the position of the Capitol, whose more precise framing geometry is shown in a drawing

Fig. 79   from Le Corbusier's office. This contains the root of the geometrical order presented below.

105

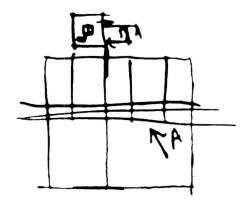

Fig. 78 Le Corbusier's first sketch for the Chandigarh concept

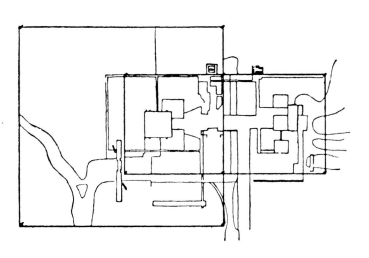

Fig. 79 The geometrical order of the Capitol, drawing by Le Corbusier

[73] Maxwell Fry in "Chandigarh, Forty Years After Le Corbusier", p. 22.

Fig. 80   A square with sides 800 m long (the breadth of one sector in the city of Chandigarh) is the initial figure for marking out the disposition of the government buildings.

Fig. 81   The corners of the square are marked ("obelisks"), and so are its central axes. It is divided into four equal horizontal strips. This produces two central squares next to each other (identified by diagonals), with one reflected outwards on the right-hand edge. The horizontal axis of the initial square is extended to the right.

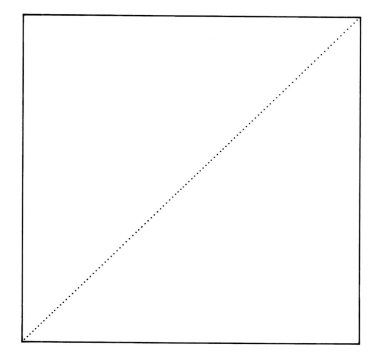

Fig. 80

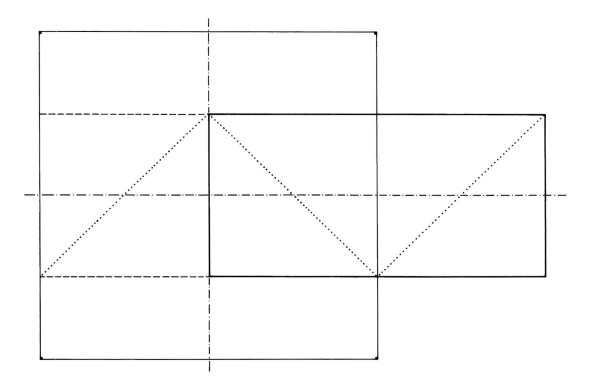

Fig. 81

Fig. 80–87 Geometrical analysis of the layout of the Capitol buildings

Fig. 82   The square reflected outwards and its left-hand neigh-
           bour form a double square with its axis on the right-
           hand edge of the initial square. This double square is
           the key frame for the arrangement of the buildings. In-
           side it is subdivided into areas by vertical lines following
           the proportions of the Golden Section. This double
           square and its divisions correspond with the anthropo-
           metric double square that Le Corbusier used for his in-
           vestigations of proportion in the "Modulor". It consists
           of a single square that generates the proportions of
           the Golden Section by projecting the diagonals of its
           half on to one side. The outline of the double square
           can be determined by the "place of the right angle" on
           the axis of the square. This is the key starting figure for
           the Modulor, with a scale of interdependent Golden
           Section values (see fig. 69), which are applied to the
           Capitol site.

Fig. 83   All the vertical divisions from the preceding double
           square figure A-B-C-D-E-G are now determined and
           allocated. Another division is created by halving the
           left-hand square. The diagonal of one of its halves pro-
           jected to the right produces the line F. The Parliament
           Building and the High Court are now placed centrally
           on the horizontal axis of the initial square and of the
           double square. The square outline of a defined dimen-
           sion of the Parliament Building is placed towards the
           left-hand edge of the double square centrally on trace
           B. Opposite this, the rectangular figure of the High
           Court, of a defined dimension, is placed with its left-
           hand edge on trace F, i. e. towards the right-hand edge
           of the double square. Thus legislature and executive
           are placed at a great distance from each other, almost
           irreconcilable, opposite each other, in a fixed position
           within the frame of the double square.[74] The horizon-
           tal axis is the link and becomes the "processional route"
           between the buildings.

[74] The original direct axial counterpart of the Parliament Building and
High Court can be seen from sketch no. 4361, Fondation Le Corbusier, Paris.

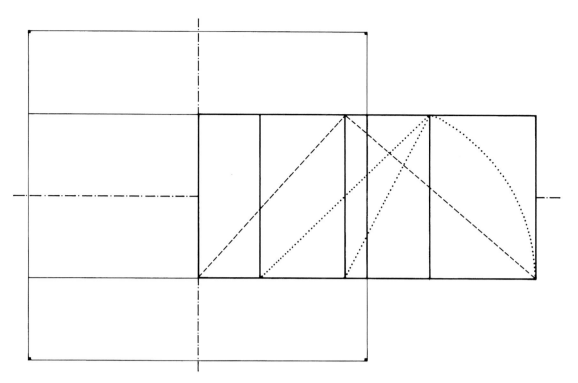

Fig. 82

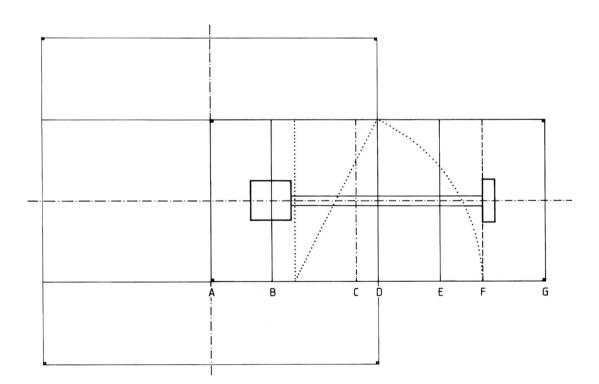

A   B   C D   E   F   G

Fig. 83

Fig. 84   This figure fixes the essential geometrical disposition of the four main buildings in the Capitol. The outline of the double square plays an important part here. This frame starts to "oscillate" in a vertical direction by a dimension X, i.e. its outlines acquire two possible readings. The width of this oscillation is also controlled by the Golden Section. This is done by using the diagonal of half the lower quarter of the 800 m initial square to construct an arc of a circle. The point at which the arc intersects with the line D at the top gives the width X, thus producing a field in the Golden Section proportion (diagonal broken line). The figure of the Governor's Palace is placed on the new top line of the double square on trace C; the palace has the breadth X, and is shifted slightly downwards. North of the palace a grid dependent on X for a Moghul garden for the governor is created between traces B and D. The width of the Parliament Building can also be derived from X: its overall breadth equals 2X. The oscillation of the horizontal axis does not just determine the outline of the Parliament Building but also establishes the main entrance to the Court, which its shifted by its width: the path from the Court to the Parliament Building deviates horizontally at a point behind axis E.

The fourth building is the long Secretariat with a set length of 250 m. It is outside the double square, but the left-hand line of the double square "slides" along its long side and is marked in the roof area. This side of the Secretariat defines the Capitol field like a wall, however without really creating space.

Fig. 85   Once more, building lines are determined by the vertical oscillation of the double square, this time in the opposite direction. The distance of shift X thus created corresponds with the "movement" upwards (on the plane of the sheet). The downward-shifting line defines first of all the bottom border of the sunken area around the Open Hand monument on trace E. The same figure shifts upwards to the left of the Governor's Palace. The Parliament Building square now starts to regulate the measurements of this two-sided shifting. The truncated pyramid sculpture is attached on its lower line – the shifted axis of the double square – on trace C. Pools outside the Governor's Palace indicate the shift, and an access line on the lower edge of the double square between traces A and C is a clear reminder of this process. The whole of the shifted field (rectangle with broken diagonals) becomes a Golden Section proportion. An incision is made into the site as an access road on vertical axis D, and this becomes a kind of geometrical directrix. Here too a line is created on the roof of the Secretariat, a kind of marker to remind us of the movement. However, the fact that the important border G on the right-hand edge of the sheet is ignored remains inexplicable. All that is planned there are steles at the corners, even though Le Corbusier probably intended to dissolve the frame here as a transition to the green area and adjacent lake. The façades of the Secretariat and the High Court border a square as a latent "superstructure".

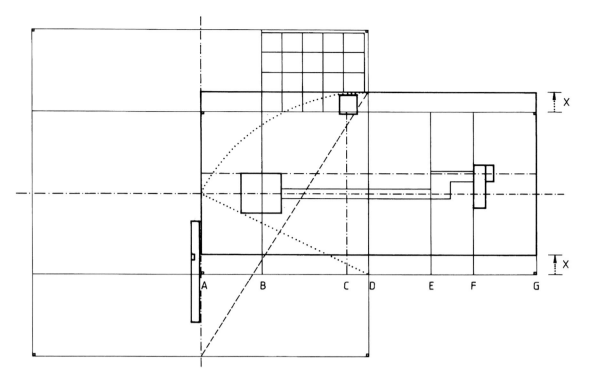

X

X

A   B   C D   E   F   G

Fig. 84

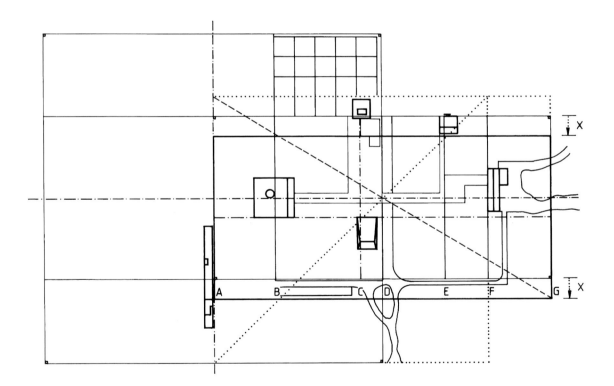

X

X

A   B   C D   E   F   G

Fig. 85

Fig. 86   Thus the most important positions for the buildings and monuments on the Capitol have been determined. The double square with the dimensions 800 by 400 m forms the frame for the arrangement, dependent on divisions in the ratio of the Golden Section. These divisions are based, as previously demonstrated, on the geometrical generation of the double square from a single square of the same length as the short side. This "mother square" with sides 400 m long (dotted diagonal) is always present in terms of its own lines, even though it is not directly perceptible to visitors to the site. The Monument to the Victims of the Partition of the Punjabi State – a ramped structure – and the Tower of the Shadows – a brise-soleil pavilion – are placed at its centre, at the intersection point of the axes. The ground plan of the pavilion is a square turned so that its side lies approximately on the trace of the diagonals described.

A variety of related pathways with lines forming secondary areas within the geometrical structure are worked out now. Pools and changes of level were intended to present a relief-like, varied surface for the site, but the reality offers an imperfect and dreary picture.

Fig. 87   Here we see a formal analogy that can illustrate Le Corbusier's unshakeable belief in the anthropomorphic proportional connections and links created by the Golden Section. Since the development of the Modulor the relationship of single and double square with the Golden Sections derived from them has played a central role in his designs. And in the Chandigarh Capitol as well the buildings are arranged on traces that – as shown – follow these divisions.

Although the chosen scale in the "magic field" at the Chandigarh Capitol climbs towards infinity, Le Corbusier still shows his firm faith in the fact that order as a transcendental dimension remains perceptible.

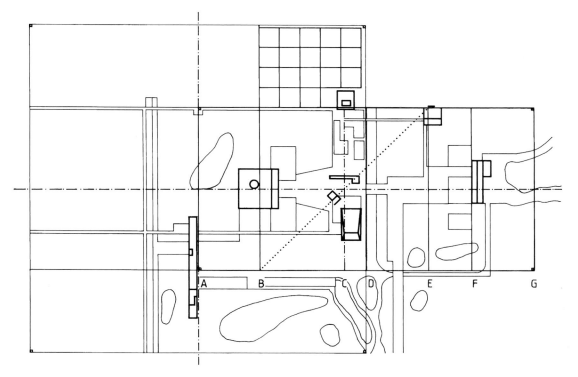

Fig. 86

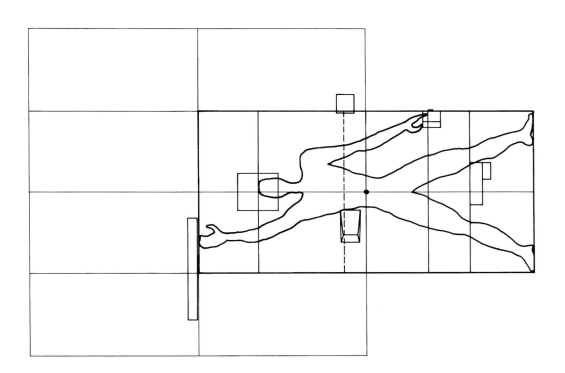

Fig. 87

Parliament Building
1952–1963 Chandigarh India

The form of the Parliament Building is determined by square and circle as plan figures and by "distorted" geometrical bodies on the roof. Even in such a general description symbolic forms emerge that appear as mediators of something sublime and dignified that reaches out beyond man. The emphatic geometry indicates metaphysical connections. As Kahn says: *"Assembly is of transcendent nature"*,[75] and in the same way Le Corbusier tries to give the primal process of people coming together to make common decisions a form that is eloquent and meaningful.

Offices are arranged on the periphery of three sides of the approximately square building; the ground floor plan is shown here. The offices are open-plan and can be subdivided as wished. Le Corbusier follows his tried-and-tested principle of separating load-bearing and cladding functions, and creates a "forest of columns" to carry the loads involved. But there is an ambiguity in the office façades with their dramatically oblique brise-soleil: the evenly spaced diagonal walls linked with carefully proportioned apertures suggest an independent façade "moving" quite separately from the building itself, but at the same time the outer lines of the diagonal walls combine with the surface of the building, flowing into each other and forming a common plane with it. In this way they are entirely in a position to perform load-bearing functions, but the viewer remains uncertain. Shifting an independent part of a building and fusing

Fig. 88

116

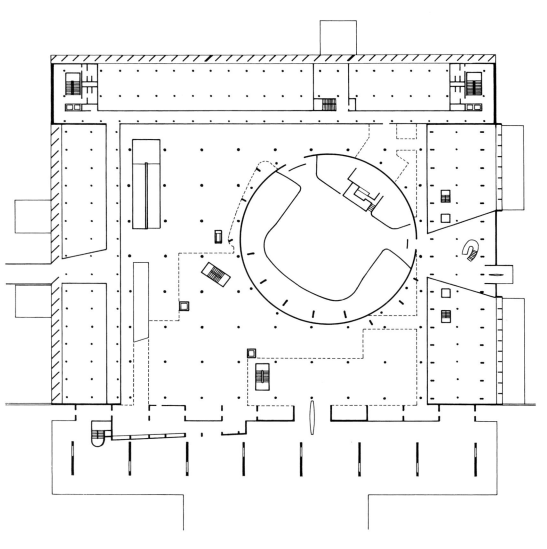

*Fig. 88 Ground floor plan of the Parliament Building
(redrawn after Le Corbusier by Klaus-Peter Gast, 1999)*

[75] Louis I. Kahn, quotation from Richard Saul Wurman, "What Will be has Always Been", New York 1986, p. 105, in the context of Kahn's design for the Parliament Building in Dhaka, Bangladesh.

• *Chandigarh, view from the pyramid*

Detail of Parliament Building with portico and roof-top structures

View from the east

Main entrance from the plaza with portico and Tower of the Shadows

Brise-soleil façades from the east

Pedestrian bridge

the surfaces form a contrasting pair that Le Corbusier is able to combine most impressively. This approach differs significantly from his earlier designs, in which he liked to contrast lively internal forms with sharp-angled and precise geometry on the outside. This brise-soleil façade for the Chandigarh Parliament is thus an innovation by Le Corbusier.

On the fourth side of the building, the actual main façade and entrance side, is the massive portico, a concrete roof supported on eight wall slabs that also functions as a gigantic gutter. This roof represents the clearest departure from the rationally devised look of Le Corbusiers buildings of the twenties. Here the hand of the subjectively designing individual is at work, as the form is a direct image of spontaneous invention. The idea is put on paper in a moment and "freezes" without any geometrical or otherwise mathematical control, and is then implemented. Even though the curvature may obey geometrical laws in places, in contrast with

creator. This is a roof structure whose heroic lines go well beyond the mere function called "roof". But: is this roof really monumental and nothing else? Its role in getting rid of rainwater is still clearly expressed in the form of a larger-than-life-size gutter. Thus a subtly ironic element creeps in, a caricature of traditional monumentalism. And the weathered concrete surface with its "aesthetic of the shabby" and its patina also contributes ultimately to making the whole thing look less sparklingly magnificent. We could go back to Eisenman[76] and suggest that this new kind of expressiveness in Le Corbusier has the quality of an exclusively self-referential sign. The widely-held interpretation that this portico relates to the High Court building opposite may be correct at first glance. But there are things that don't add up: the two buildings are enormously far apart, over 400 m, and so scarcely communicate with each other – anyone who has visited the site will agree with that –; also the entrance axis to the Court is clearly

Le Corbusier's painting on the entrance door

Walls of the portico

earlier designs, the Capitol buildings are the first evidence that Le Corbusier, in parallel with the development of the Ronchamp chapel, is entertaining the thought of using "irrational form". Even the structures on the roof of the Villa Savoye are clearly subject to a geometrical order that presents itself to the outside world. Something that had been suggested previously in the structures on top of the Unité d'Habitation in Marseilles – especially the chimneys – becomes the defining gesture here. "Free", uncalculated form comes to the fore, and with it the personality, the "singularity", of the designer. This fact represents one of the greatest differences between this and Le Corbusier's early work. But it does not bring about a "break". The roof of the portico is no longer a *prescribed* form, that is to say predetermined in its form by geometry, but it is also not a fundamentally new form. It is not calling on the formal stock of history, it is not registering a claim to universal form, but simply celebrating the intuitive strength of its

shifted, and not least, the curve of the roof points upwards. The roof's gesture thrusts out – or is it actually inviting us in? – and tries to make the sky relate to this viewpoint from the portico as a "backdrop" or setting for natural phenomena. Human legislature, embodied in the Parliament Building, meets the power of nature at the portico, which serves as a linking element. The power of nature is faced with a massive field that has been assigned to it on earth, the Capitol terrain between the Parliament and the Court. A plateau as a meeting-place between man and God. It is at this point in the whole composition of the building, at the point of the portico, that Le Corbusier's interest in a metaphysical reference in terms of "accessibility" comes clearly to the fore. This is additionally supported by nature symbols like sun, rain, lightning behind the portico, and also animal figures on the entrance portal. Perhaps the intention is that man the law-giver should be made aware of his relative role in the events of the world

[76] Eisenman, "La Maison Dom-ino ...".

120

*Detail of the portico and
the lateral façade*

View from the pyramid

Separation of vehicular and pedestrian traffic

when faced with all-powerful nature, captured in the symbols of the portal.

The entrance portal – at least this was Le Corbusier's intention – was to be opened once a year by the Governor to mark the beginning of the new parliamentary session. But in fact it has not been used in the past 25 years. Members of the Assembly and visitors use various side entrances to get into the impressive but rather dark hall, which is such a contrast with the dazzling light outside. The hall leads to the two main rooms, which follow the British model, the upper and the lower house, inserted into the building's interior as independent volumes. The smaller chamber is lit by a skylight in the shape of a tetrahedron, while the lower house widens at the top in a shape reminiscent of a cooling tower. The bevelled line of this tower contains an elaborate mechanical lighting system and is intended to provide the chamber with natural light according to requirements. Le Corbusier gave a great deal of thought to this system, but it is hardly ever used. Problems arise from the acoustics, so the use of the chamber itself is restricted, although von Moos[77] suggests that this chamber is one of the few real parliamentary spaces created by modern architecture. It is circular, countering the square outline of the building around it. Two "ears", called "Ladies' Galleries" in the ground plan provide banks of seats and are appended as rooms with free forms. Otherwise all the ground plan figurations are right-angled and the wall slabs of the outer façade, described above, are placed diagonally. The journalists' area is carefully separated from the areas used by members. So Le Corbusier's recurring motif of "soft", flowing forms and hard outer lines is to be found in the Parliament Building, but it is counterpointed here by the geometrically developed circle of the chamber. It is quite rigid, and carries associations with movement within the ground plan only in terms of its asymmetrical and yet carefully calculated position. Generous galleries on the first floor level with ventilation spaces between them provide for variations of spatial structures on the vertical plane as well.

The sculptural drama of the Parliament Building's rooftop structures is not only intended to indicate that this is the most important building in the Capitol precinct, but it also refers to another dimension that has been mentioned above. The truncated paraboloid of the Assembly chamber is a light-capturing device that stretches up to the sky. Cooling towers are not the only influence here. Brooks[78] has proved convincingly that the chimney of a Jura farmhouse near La Chaux-de-Fonds, Le Corbusier's birthplace, contributed as well. The bevelled effect and a sliding cover that was originally planned but abandoned on grounds of cost are reminiscent of this type of chimney with an obliquely placed opening flap. This double formal borrowing is now transformed into a magic object. It is not just the aperture itself, but the autonomous structures on top of it that make this "skylight" into an instrument for communicating between earth and heaven, between the real and the transcendental world. This function as an "aerial" is enhanced by linking it via a metallic and transparent bridge to a towering lift-shaft that is also bevelled, and whose walls also form an independent figure as a sculpture. It becomes a "transmission mast", and with the point pyramidal roof of the second Assembly chamber is an instrument for communication with the world beyond. Thus the roof-top structures and the Capitol plateau belong together, and their dimensions and disposition can be understood only through the allegory described. Le Corbusier's profoundly romantic soul, which is closely bound up with all-embracing nature, is intensely reflected in the metaphysical and monumental expressiveness of the architecture of his Parliament Building in Chandigarh.

The surface of the building, which is still in good structural condition, looks rough and coarse. The béton brut, which originally gleamed white in India's dazzling light, has acquired a blackish-grey surface in the course of time, a patina with an aesthetic of its own. The ingratiating character of the white prisms of the twenties is now faced with an astringent material aesthetic that is not immediately accessible to the eye. Le Corbusier says that its natural quality is intended to come close to that of stone. But the assertive presence of this patina seems overpowering alongside the rough quality of the execution. "Ignobility" lacks "nobility" as a counterpart, at least as a suggestion.

And so the Indians experience their architecture as something to be taken for granted, or perhaps they find that it is too much for them. They receive, but scarcely perceive it. The soldiers' tents hang like spiders' webs between the wall slabs of the portico, in an ignorance that is almost loveable. The architecture is simply there, and its heroic gesture produces no genuflections.

[77] Von Moos, "Le Corbusier", p. 320.
[78] Brooks, "Le Corbusier's Formative Years", pp. 186–191.

Assembly chamber (upper house)

Assembly chamber (lower house)

Fig. 89   The geometry of the Parliament Building is based on a square of a defined size. As has already been shown in the analysis of the overall Capitol complex, the dimensions of the Parliament Building relate directly to the measurements that lie behind the site as a whole, 2 times 800 m, and then arising from this 2 times 400 m, with its proportional derivations.

Fig. 90   A second, larger square of a defined size is assigned to the initial square with its axes and its centre. Its right-hand outer trace lies on the right-hand side of the first square. These "primary settings" provide a basis for determining the position of the subsequent plan figures. The position of the round section of the building for the chamber can be determined only by precisely establishing the outer lines produced by the two squares.

Fig. 91   Here we see that the placing of the chamber circle arises directly from the interplay of the two squares. The Golden Section divisions of each of the two squares are crucially important (GS). A small strip is produced between these divisions, and its central axis precisely defines the position of the circle horizontally. A diagonal of a square (dotted line) now also combines the two squares that establish the outline: the axis of the circle as mediator between the two Golden Section divisions meets the outer line of the larger square at the bottom, and from this intersection the diagonal meets the smaller square on its left-hand outer line. Here it is possible to add a horizontal line that intersects with the vertical axis of the circle, forming its horizontal axis and thus defining the position of the circle exactly.

Fig. 89–94: Ground plan analysis of the Parliament Building

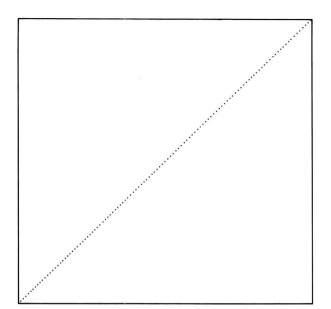

Fig. 89

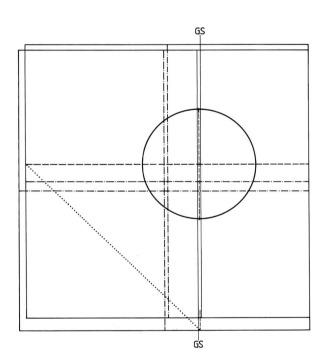

Fig. 90

Fig. 91

Fig. 92   Another square of a defined size is inscribed centrally within the initial square from figure 89 (dotted line); the lines of this new square define the lines of the office area on the outer periphery. Peripheral zones of various widths are created by overlapping with the second square from figure 90. Differently shaped access areas are separated off on three sides in the area of the axis lines of the first two squares and the circle. This ring encloses an inner square zone with a corridor system, thus producing a hall with the body of the chamber inserted into it.

Fig. 93   A grid system of a defined size is inscribed in the inner hall zone; its position depends on the geometry of the circle. This grid consists of a 8 by 7 pattern of fields, with access ramps placed on the left-hand edge within one field area. The result is a square grid separated by the ramp zone. Square access zones ("cores") are developed at the corners of the office zones, so that each of the three sides forms an independent "track". The portico, the main access area, comes into being on the southern edge of the ring, developed by a subdivision of the space into seven square fields dependent on the width of the ring. The geometry of the two initial squares is increasingly blurred by ambivalent relations of their outlines.

Fig. 94   The square grid in the hall determines the position of columns that support the roof and the galleries (shown here: the main access level from the square). A system of corridors runs round the hall and leads to the entrances and exits.

This step explains the difference in overlap between the outlines of the first two squares. Diagonal wall slabs of different widths are placed between their traces. This is the clearest indication of the presence of the square geometry that generated the ground plan. In the portico area the widths of the massive wall slabs are set apart by the proportions of the Golden Section. From the dimensions of the free-standing walls with the vaulted roof above them emerges the ground-plan projection of the roof's external lines.

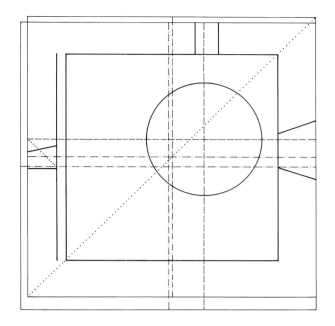

Fig. 92

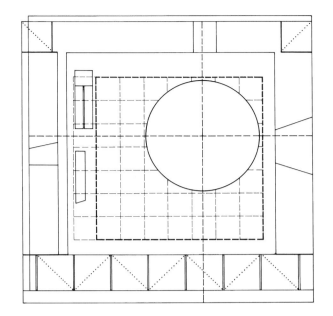

Fig. 93

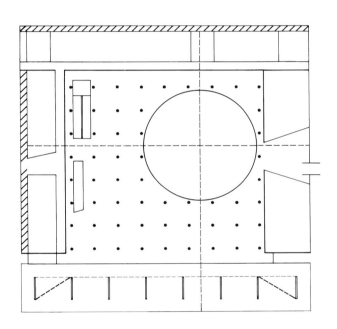

Fig. 94

High Court
1952–1956   Chandigarh   India

Fig. 95 The High Court was the first building to be completed. It was opened in 1956. It contains a row of eight courtrooms on ground floor level and a main courtroom separated from the others by a large entrance hall. A restaurant, a library and other side rooms are accommodated in a rear, lower part of the building.

The predominant character of the building is created by a double effect: the first impression is of a dominant box frame, establishing a rectangular block as a figure, before any functional considerations emerge. But then massive vaulted arches can be seen below the line of the box frame which span between the clearly articulated dividing walls of the courtrooms. Then the next moment you realize that these arches make up the whole roof, and that the "frame" is merely a suggestion, a line that has to link the two walls of the short sides. Two formal and constructional techniques that are almost opposites, the frame and the arch, are fused into a hybrid form that makes it possible to perceive them as both at the same time. Like a puzzle picture, first one impression is dominant, and then the other. Below the arches, a sharp edge cuts off the roofline of the courtrooms, and indicates by means of a convex shape that something has been "inserted" here. The façade figure of the courtrooms tends towards achieving independence: the curve also means detachment from the frame and from the structure associated with it. Additionally, the façade figure of the courtrooms is interrupted by the incision made by the monumental entrance area, in which two gigantic walls are placed, with rounded ends and tapering in ground plan towards the middle. They unmistakably proclaim the "main entrance", but this is essentially an exercise in prestige, as the drive and thus the main access are at the back of the building. In contrast with the walls pointing into the depths of the building there is a barrier: the ramps as a transverse pedestrian access element. It is a dividing element within the depths of the space, confronting the depth and also gently transforming the movement into the depths into the vertical dimension, referring functionally to the access level of the courtrooms and finally, it is simply a free-standing sculpture as well.

All the above-mentioned parts that make their impact in the front view form their own "planes", which then relate by being "layered" behind one another. The façade of the courtrooms – almost decoratively devalued as an independent brise-soleil honeycomb structure –

curves upwards to indicate that it "wants" to be independent. It actually consists of two planes, the brise-soleil pattern and the window level. Both are effectively independent of each other, but yet closely linked. They are related via the ordering structure of the courtroom partition walls to the plane of the arches far behind. The honeycomb structure, a bordering layer with apparent depth, is clearly legible as a plane on the outside. This means that the abrupt break created by the entrance dramatizes a sudden enormous increase in depth of this plane and produces a contrast of staggered layers and immediate depth. The massive walls effect a transition from one principle to another, inevitably drawing the viewer's eye into the depths. Thus the façade organization of the High Court is characterized by the fact that its parts are independent and at the same time linked with the whole, by building up layers paired with in-depth penetration of these layers. The various layers – of the frame, the brise-soleil with the outline of the three wall slabs, the layer of the plane of glass, the arches at their deepest point and finally the ramp layer – form an overlapping system, penetrate each other without destroying each other. In Hoesli's[79] words, the façade of the High Court establishes *"transparency in the figurative sense"*.

This extremely complex façade structure contradicts the organization of the ground plan to a certain extent. The plan's rigidity and additive structure suggest a simple build-up without any spatial complexity. The only meaningful overlap area for façade and interior is at the barrier formed by the ramp, which attempts to enrich the enormous depth of the entrance hall by establishing a new line, a transversely placed, perforated plane. However, it is not able to build up a subtle structure, but merely indicates the rear access zone, which runs transversely to it at that point and connects the deep hall with the narrow corridor running at right angles to it. This less than complex ground plan structure suggests that Le Corbusier left an assistant to develop the ground plan, having conceived the idea, while going on to design the façades himself. A different theory is that the low rear section of the building was added later. But it is clear even in early sketches that the L-shaped building was present as a concept from the outset. Le Corbusier separates the courtrooms and the other functions, without detaching them, and adds a secondary building to the main body for the rear entrance. The false impression of a section added at a later date given by the secondary building could support the suggestion of "outside work" on the ground plan by an assistant.

128

79 Hoesli, in Rowe and Slutzky, "Transparency", new edition, commentary pp. 64–69.

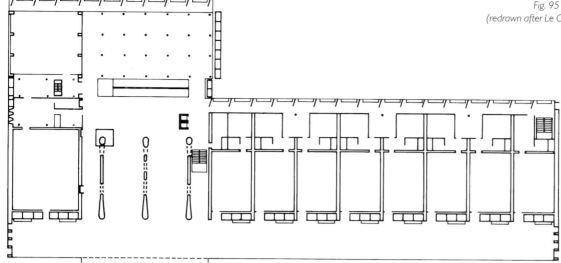

*Fig. 95 Ground floor plan of the High Court
(redrawn after Le Corbusier by Klaus-Peter Gast, 1999)*

High Court from the Plaza

Main entrance with free-standing wall

View from the area in front of the High Court

The first sketches show that Le Corbusier had a "final shape" in mind at a very early stage, as with the other buildings in the Capitol, and that all he had to do was develop the nuances. In the Capitol buildings in particular, it is very striking that form is often found through an *idea*. It is not so much a continuous process of genesis that is to the fore, in other words the continuing development of an original thought that the final design could depart from considerably, but an inspiration that is spontaneously seen to be correct and appropriate. Le Corbusier astonishingly trusts his inspiration to the extent that it is not subjected to any major change. He gives enormous weight to the spontaneously "frozen" idea, so that ultimately there is a danger that formalism arising from emotion or even subjectively minted figures or part-figures could be allowed to dominate. The façade of the High Court consists of an accumulation of such independent individual figures of a strongly subjective character. Vaulted arches, rounded wall slabs, an expressive, forward-leaning wall formation and the brise-soleil pattern are all design figures that could make things difficult for any one of the others. The resultant heterogeneity does not make the façade disintegrate,

but could easily give the impression that the elements compete with each other. The above-mentioned transparency in a transferred sense, as formulated by Hoesli after Rowe/Slutzky, is evoked by a heterogeneous ensemble here, and no longer, as was so excellently demonstrated earlier by the Villa Stein, by homogeneous component figures derived from a common family of forms. This is one of the most remarkable differences between Chandigarh and Le Corbusier's architecture in the twenties.

The heterogeneous nature of autonomous component figures, as for example in the arch structure of the roof, leads to contradictory impressions. Similarly to the portico of the Parliament, the large roof, conceived as a screen, opens on to the wide area between the two buildings, and to the sky. One drawing by Le Corbusier does not put the roof in the foreground so much as the effect of a picture being "framed" by the outline of the High Court, a picture of the expansive terrain, populated in the drawing, with its solitary monuments. This idea of a clearly framing outline from the perspective of the upper storey, which is the view that those working in the Court would have, seems to have been

Fig. 96

Fig. 96 Le Corbusier's sketch of the view of the Capitol square from the High Court

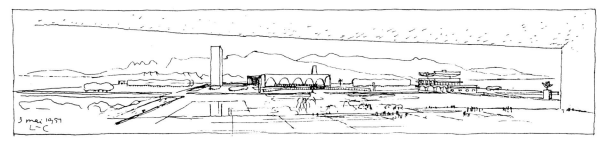

Brise-soleil in the main façade

Roof terrace with opening to the Parliament Building

Free-standing walls in the main entrance

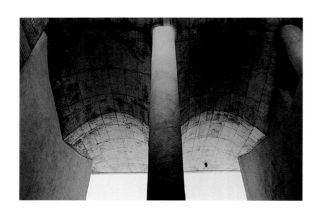

Drive side

Drive side

important to Le Corbusier. It is idealized, as so often. Neither the lively coming and going, and thus "enjoyment" of the area, nor the dimensions of this representation correspond with the reality of a precinct for the legislature and the executive that was remote and scarcely used by the general public. The huge shifts in scale that we see in Le Corbusier's drawings from his early villa designs onwards reveal his desire for wideopen spaces and thus a sense of splendour that is often a far cry from the built reality. Inside the frame, the roof vaulting certainly emphasizes its own importance as a screen against rain and sun, but mainly it is a demonstration of engineering skill rather than a function being fulfilled. And even this is not completely true: the bold form of the spherical double-shell concrete arches is impressive, but they are not load-bearing, and thus alien to the engineer's fundamentally structural approach. Le Corbusier is using "form for form's sake" here, and transforming the classical arch – even the classical Indian arch – into a self-referential, autonomous figuration. Even more than the key-patterned brisesoleil, this use of arches has an autonomous character that is essentially subjective, and thus seems mannered. Additionally, this shield has a protective function only in the upper storeys and the entrance hall, as the courtrooms themselves have their own roofs, which is emphasized by the protruding parapet. Thus the roof's meaning goes beyond these "functions". Similarly to the portico of the Parliament Building, this roof is intended to give a sense of broadening out to the plateau and to the sky. And a transcendental connection could also be intended in the High Court, though it does not seem as obvious as in the Parliament Building. The following analysis shows that Le Corbusier did in fact design the ground plan on the basis of ordering principles that refer symbolically to transcendental connections. The analytical sequence of the ground plan of the entrance level from the plateau shows that the entrance hall is the key to the geometrical connections. Here we can see the influence of the insights gained from the Modulor about the Golden Section as a result of linking single and double squares, as has already been shown for the Capitol site as a whole.

The entrance hall to the High Court consists of a double square of a defined size. This is the determining initial figure for the analysis of geometry and scale.

Fig. 97

Within the double square, major emphasis is put on those lines that result from the process of geometrical derivation of the double square from the single square (see figs. 66 to 68). The derivations from the Golden Section thus generated form the basis for sets of ground plan lines that determine the whole layout. The centre line of the double square is shown broken as an aid to orientation.

Fig. 98

Divisions of the double square area produced by geometrical construction reveal that the lines of the component figures in the entrance hall determine all other lines – and thus spaces. The centre line of the double square C establishes the rear limit of the courtrooms. Thus, together with the line of the "place of the right angle" D, an area for ancillary rooms is created along the entrances to the courtrooms. The central line B of the ramp fixes the position of the ramp. Its width is determined by dividing off a square space top left dependent on A. This also fixes the final width of the main courtroom with the zone for ancillary rooms. Line E as a line belonging to the initial square borders the courtrooms in the main façade on the plane of their windows, and F finally sets the line of the roof frame.

Fig. 99

Fig. 97

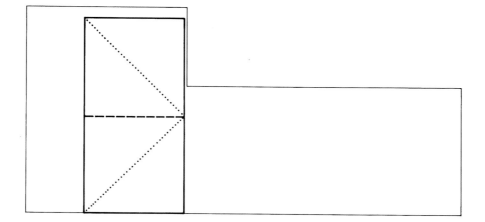

Fig. 98

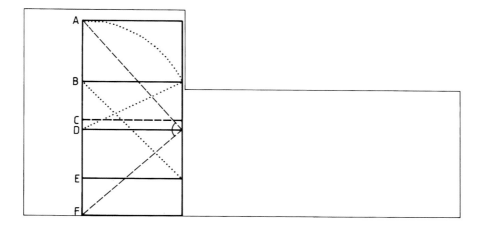

Fig. 99

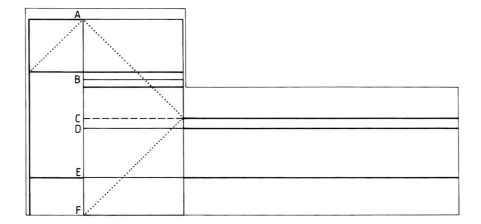

Fig. 97–101 Ground plan analysis of the High Court

Fig. 100   Shifting the single initial square by a distance of a defined size confirms both the lower line of the ramp and the external limit of the brise-soleil, which protects the rooms from the sun. The curves of the three wall slabs inside the entrance lie on this line. Their rear limit is determined by the middle line of the double square (broken). Similar to the analysis of the distortion process used on the round columns in the Villa Stein (see figs. 33/34), it becomes clear at this point why Le Corbusier chose this tear-drop shape for the end of walls. The distortion process of the shifting square is frozen within them. Thinning down towards the middle and broadening at the end shows the dynamic process of *stretching*. Movement and distortion are thus built into the geometrical genesis of the plan.

The initial square from which the double square is generated also plays a crucial part in setting the dimensions of the courtrooms. It develops the line of the main courtroom on the left. It is applied to the right of the entrance hall at a distance of a wall thickness of a defined size and fixes the width of a total of three courtrooms. During this process internal spatial lines are generated in the ratio of the Golden Section (strong broken line). Once this area figure has been established it is finally used to determine the eight rooms and the right-hand wall of the building.

Fig. 101   Thus all the major ground plan lines in the High Court are developed geometrically. A side-room zone is divided off in the access area to the rooms at the back. This zone is determined by individual outlines in the proportions of the Golden Section. This sets the rear façade depth for the full length of the diagonally placed brise-soleil.

136

Fig. 100

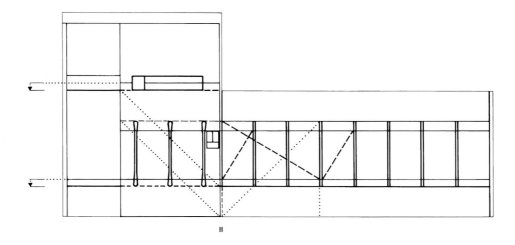

II

Fig. 101

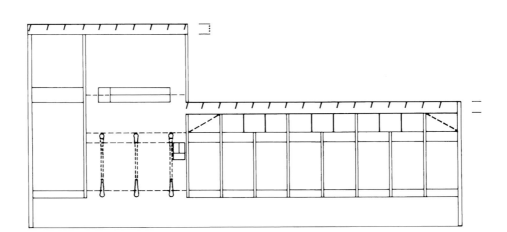

Secretariat
1952–1958   Chandigarh   India

The largest building within the Capitol ensemble is the Secretariat, an administrative complex 254 m long and 41 m high. Le Corbusier's original intention was to build a tower modelled on his skyscraper design for Algeria in 1941, but there were to be no skyscrapers in Chandigarh. So he quickly pulled an alternative suggestion out of his pocket, which was realized almost completely in its first version.

The horizontal block consists of six eight-storey sections for different administrative functions. One part is intended for office space for ministers and the governor. As can be seen from a first glance at the Secretariat building, Le Corbusier marks the ministers' sec-

fitted into a composition here that draws life from the special sections: the ministerial section, an almost closed ramp structure on both sides and the carefully considered roof-top structures. The office façade becomes a "background" for individually featured elements, which thus make a particular impact. We will mention only in passing that the projecting ramps represent an error of judgement in terms of functionality; they more probably arise from the intention of adding a contrasting closed section to the design. It is also not clear whether the façade or the ground plan of the ministerial section was designed first, as the independent play of the façade suggests a dimension of reference that is independent of the plan.

As in the other Capitol buildings, the aesthetic of the concrete with a patina seems over-assertive, especially as the Secretariat was built very carelessly, which produced some extremely crude surfaces and details. The precisely drawn line and the smooth, even surface are

140

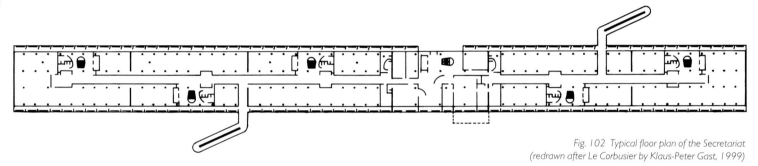

Fig. 102 Typical floor plan of the Secretariat
(redrawn after Le Corbusier by Klaus-Peter Gast, 1999)

tion with an elaborate brise-soleil composition. As the whole block acquired a uniform balcony façade, the distinguished design for this section was not only welcome but necessary, as otherwise the building would have become entirely monotonous. The ministers' rooms were conceived two-storeyed in part, which allowed some design leeway. But this also led – as in the façade pattern for the High Court – to an impression of a façade that has been devalued decoratively: the relative freedom produced a façade that is arranged randomly and thus entirely self-referential, with which Le Corbusier is "playing". On the one hand, in the normal offices, faith in functionality is celebrated, as the same content should be expressed in the same way in the façade. But then concentrating energy on the ministerial block seems too strained and contrived. And yet the façade of this section is certainly impressive, and tries to link up with the rest of the structure on both sides. Le Corbusier also used this uniform façade structure of floor slabs with external supports and detached balcony walls in central buildings in the city, and so it became a typical Chandigarh motif. While this pattern turns out to be genuinely monotonous in the town it is

missing as a contrast: they would have helped the concrete, rough from its shuttering, to look more dignified. The patina aesthetic is present everywhere and strains the eye, which is unable to find a brief moment of respite.

In the centre of the building is an excavation one storey deep, where the main entrance is placed. A two-storey "gap" can be seen approximately in the middle of the entrance area, making it possible to drive through the building to the area at the back. However, we shall never know whether Le Corbusier planned an extension on this site, which already has the necessary infrastructure in place.

The typical floor plan is a simple pattern of offices that can be subdivided as wished arranged symmetrically on both sides of a central corridor. Large open-plan offices are formed at each end. In the following analysis of its geometrical build-up we will show how Le Corbusier structured this simple plan, so well established for office use.

The Secretariat is often called the "boundary wall" of the site, but this is not really the point. As can be seen from fig. 77 (full general plan), the area behind the Sec-

Fig. 102

Secretariat with the Parliament Building portico front right

Entrance area

retariat was marked out with "obelisks" (Le Corbusier), which here means border markings, but these were unfortunately never put in place. They define the geometrical boundary, the actual area of the plateau, which is determined by the regular breadth of a sector of the town. Here the idea of an extension – whatever it might have been for – rears its head, because of the developed area behind the Secretariat. But as far as conveying the geometry of the Capitol buildings as realized is concerned, the Secretariat is a "track" along which the ordering figure "glides" (see figs. 84–86). This also makes the length of the building comprehensible, as it is needed to perform this task.

Seen in the context of the Capitol's ordering figures, the dimensions of the Secretariat refer to transcendental matters we have already mentioned, meanings that cannot be perceived as such. As a real building it seems too large, absolutely gigantic, in comparison with the other architecture. But read as a sign of excessively large scale, the Secretariat does have its own validity, as a reference to the Capitol complex's transcendental plane of reference. This seems to provide the most plausible explanation for its enormous dimensions.

Le Corbusier was certainly pleased to take the opportunity to plan a building as large as this but – and this is an irony of fate – it is far too small to fulfil its function properly. Dividing the state into Punjab and Hariyana meant that twice the amount of administration was needed. The building now houses three times the number of employees that was planned, some of whom are forced out on to the balconies, which have been converted into offices.

View from the drive to the Capitol

Military camp on the edge of the Capitol site

Detail of the concrete with traces of rough shuttering

Corner design for the loggias and ramp sculpture

Dining-room on the roof with ramp volume in front

Ministers' offices with ramp and viewing point on the roof

Access road to the Secretariat

Fig. 103 The basic form of the Secretariat is predetermined as a long rectangle. The length of the building was largely determined by the quantity of space needed. A central axis sets the position of the corridor.

Fig. 104 Six parts of the rectangle form the individual administrative sections. Their dimensions are predetermined: sections 1, 2 and 6 are the same length, 3 and 5 are larger units and 4 has its own special dimensions as part of the accommodation for ministers.

Fig. 105 A double square, projected over the central axis on to the rectangle, is now derived from the length of the rectangle. The double square as a suggestive figure does not determine the edge of the building. It is however crucial in establishing the internal structure of the rectangle. Its vertical central axis, the dividing line between the squares, established the first wall position within the rectangle.

Fig. 106 The construction of the double square from the single square and the resultant pattern of Golden Section divisions, as already described in the Modulor, is transferred to the figure of the rectangle. Here the key lines of the proportional figures establish positions within the ground plan structure. Together with the dividing lines of the administrative sections and the central line of the double square they create the rhythm of the plan.

Fig. 107 The side lines of the single square derived from figure 106, from which the double square is generated geometrically, finally determine the position of the two access ramps. Relating to the double square, these lines form Golden Section ratios of the part of the square involved in each case. Half of each section of the double square, in other words each quarter of the double square, establishes the position of plan figures like access steps and special rooms. These divisions trigger an even rhythm of wide and narrow fields. Centre lines can now be drawn within the wide fields. These form double squares in their turn, and establish the depth of the Secretariat rectangle as a newly established dimension X. The narrow fields, as the distance between the Golden Section of the part-square and its half fix the length of the ramps.

Fig. 108 Important ground plan positions have thus been defined. The dividing walls and the access figures, and also the dimensions of the open-plan rooms at the ends can be derived geometrically in this way.

Le Corbusier again uses the ordering figure of the proportionally divided double square when designing the Secretariat.

Fig. 103–108 Ground plan analysis of the Secretariat

Fig. 103

Fig. 104

Fig. 105

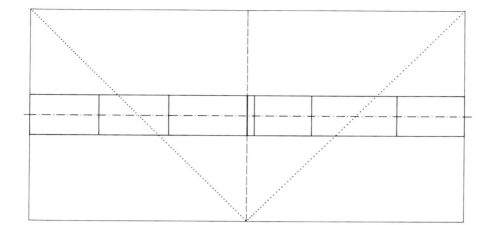

Fig. 106

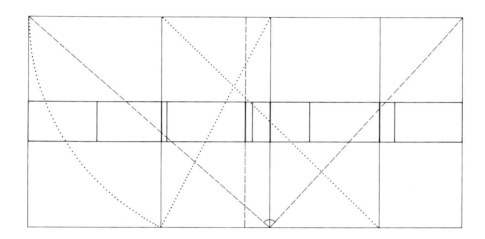

145

Fig. 107

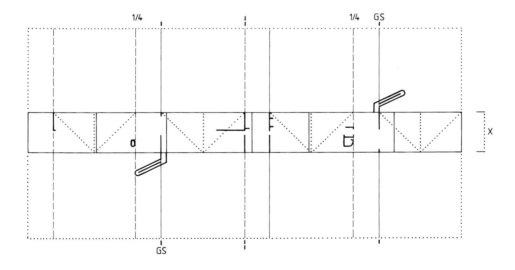

Fig. 108

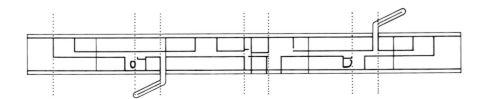

Governor's Palace
1952 Project

Le Corbusier's idea of giving the state governor a "palace" of his own in a central and therefore prestigious position did not meet with the approval of Prime Minister Nehru. The project was finally rejected as too undemocratic – and one has to understand how keen India was at the time to establish an exemplary democracy – after three years of discussion and planning. Le Corbusier' over-hasty counter-proposal for building a Museum of Knowledge based on the electronic media instead of the Governor's seat was accepted at first, and the foundation walls were actually built. Later, after Le Corbusier's death, there was neither the assertive ability nor the resources to be able to pursue the project further.

Le Corbusier must have chosen the notion of a governor's "palace" ("Le palais du gouverneur") intentionally, although the French contains various different nuances. Palace evokes the palaces of the princely rulers who were always ready to rule violently, especially in northern India. Perhaps it was this historical echo that Nehru particularly disliked, and that is understandable when one sees the opulent appointments for the building and its surrounding garden. Le Corbusier's intention is further clarified by the extraordinarily confident lines of the Governor's building, and its position on a key site confirms the impression that Le Corbusier wanted to create a kind of prestigious seat for a ruler. Le Corbusier was certainly not interested in the politically explosive aura of a building of this kind, he simply wanted to create expressive and innovative architecture.

The fact the Governor's Palace – or the museum – is missing from the Capitol site is the most painful loss for the composition as a whole. The carefully selected asymmetrical position between the Parliament Building and the High Court, approached centrally via the access road, would have tied these two buildings, which are a very long way apart, much more firmly together. Only this final point, seen against the lively landscape of the mountains would have made the plateau open to perception as a coherent place. Taken with the sculpture of the Open Hand, even on this overlarge scale it would have been perfectly clear that here a border area was being defined. The placing of the façades, with Parliament Building and High Court on the side and the Governor's Palace and the Open Hand directly accessible, would have contributed to this sense of outline. The project included a basement floor with rear ac-

cess, an entrance floor with hall and representative rooms and a gallery level, and then above this the governor's accommodation on two levels. A two-storey roof level indicates Le Corbusier's intention to hold meetings and banquets in the open air – possibly under the starry sky. In this context the shape of a stand to provide seating, which also provides shelter, is a striking feature. Curtis[80] derives this figure from the horns of Indian water buffaloes, as found in Le Corbusier's sketchbook, but it seems doubtful that it should be pinned down so firmly. In fact this motif of a figure curved through various radii appears in numerous variations, for example in the portico cross-section of the Parliament Building or in ground plan patterns as well. The figure is fixed as an idea for the project even in the earliest sketches, thus establishing itself as an important motif to the end. And so the building intended for the governor also contains a gesture of opening up to the infinite space above, and turns out to be another instrument of metaphorical reference, and one of rare clarity. In the decade after the design was created the shading function of the floating, self-detaching roof figure entered international architecture as a banal "flying roof" and became the mark of a fashion.

The distinction between the public zone below and the private residence above is marked by a "notch", a setback storey. This creates a new figure in Le Corbusier's work, the "building above a building": the ground floor is made broader and given a kind of portico, similarly to the Parliament Building, but here in the form of a brisesoleil in front, once more used decoratively by Le Corbusier. With the floating umbrella roof, this forms a kind of pyramidal hierarchy that is particularly impressive in its effect and gives a sense of succinctness to the design as a whole. The façade of the upper, "floating" section for the governor's accommodation is soberly limited to incised rectangular apertures, some of them running round the corners and giving the prismatic block its sculptural shape. This is faintly reminiscent of the Villa Savoye with its flat prism on set-back supports – on all sides, in the present case.

In this design, Le Corbusier shapes the supporting columns as cruciform, extraordinarily succinct piers. They form an approximately square grid that rises into the upper storeys and makes it possible for the dividing walls to be arranged freely. On the upper floor we then find curved non-load-bearing walls as well, a good illustration of the reliable principle of separating the functions of load-bearing and covering.

Le Corbusier surrounds the projected building with a magnificently designed exterior space with pools and changes of level in the form of steps, ramps and galleries. This modulation of the site is an important com-

Fig. 109

[80] Curtis, "Le Corbusier, Ideas and Forms", p. 193.

ponent of the Capitol plateau as a whole and was ultimately carried out only fragmentarily. What is more, Le
Corbusier also overestimated the regional attitude to
the maintenance and care of exterior spaces. Things
that have been planned and realized usually remain in
their early stages without any further care, so that even
if these plans were being realized today a somewhat
reduced impression would probably have been made.
This is confirmed by some of the gardens that actually
were completed, which today eke out an extremely
wretched existence.

In the area behind the palace, Le Corbusier intended
to plan lavish gardens reminiscent of the square patterns of Mogul gardens. But we can see that the huge
dimensions of the gardens are intended to pick up the
latently present geometrical outline of the 800 m area,
which was to have been marked out with "obelisks".
This line is the actual north-eastern border before the
foothills of the Himalayas start to rise.

The geometrical structure is present in the design for
the Governor's Palace as well. The following analytical
sequence reveals the connections between the most
important lines.

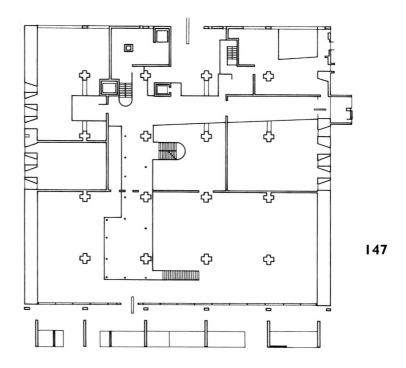

147

*Fig. 109 Gallery floor plan of the Governor's Palace
(redrawn after Le Corbusier by Klaus-Peter Gast, 1999)*

Governor's Palace, model view

Fig. 110 A square of a defined size is the initial figure for the design.

Fig. 111 The square shifts in a horizontal direction by defined distance X. This width X provides the dimensions for the multi-shell outer wall of two opposite sides of the palace. The vertical central axis can now be established for the full breadth of the building.

Fig. 112 The initial square in its original position (dotted diagonal) is now divided in the ratio of the Golden Section in both directions (bold broken line). The vertical Golden Section line becomes the orientation axis for arranging the position of the piers. This produces a left-hand field divided into three equal widths, and a narrower right-hand field that is divided into two equal widths and comprises the shifted distance X from figure 111. The dotted vertical divisions represent the vertical positions of the piers; the spacing on the right is slightly wider.

148

Fig. 113 Within the figure to the right of the Golden Section, square spacings now establish the horizontal positions of the piers across the full width. Thus the design process generates equal horizontal spacings, but unequal vertical spacings for the piers. Another Golden Section division of the half on the right of the central axis (GS2) establishes the right-hand trace of the cruciform piers and thus the width of the piers.

Fig. 114 The positions and dimensions of the piers are thus determined geometrically. Starting with the pier bottom right, it is now possible to project a square area on to the corner. The horizontal trace that this establishes marks the inner limit of the portico's free-standing walls. The outer line of the portico is established by projecting the square diagonals on to one side of the square (1 to root 2 proportion).

In this design the square chosen as a starting figure does not retain its original "pure" geometry, but is "deformed" – as for the Parliament Building. Le Corbusier does not leave the purely geometrical form in its rigid starting condition, but "dynamizes" it. Rigidity and dynamics form a closely linked pair of opposites, which is a particular feature of Le Corbusier's architecture. The deformation invokes a meaningful process of movement that creates dynamic tension in the designs. The slightly different distances between the piers in the Governor's Palace also illustrate this point, with the area proportion of the Golden Section called upon as another factor creating dynamic movement. Plan analysis reveals these powerfully dynamic processes in Le Corbusier's work for the first time, and demonstrates them visually.

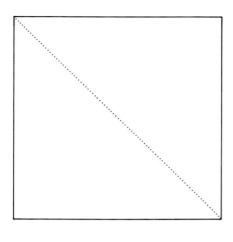

Fig. 110

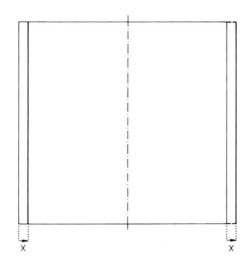

Fig. 111

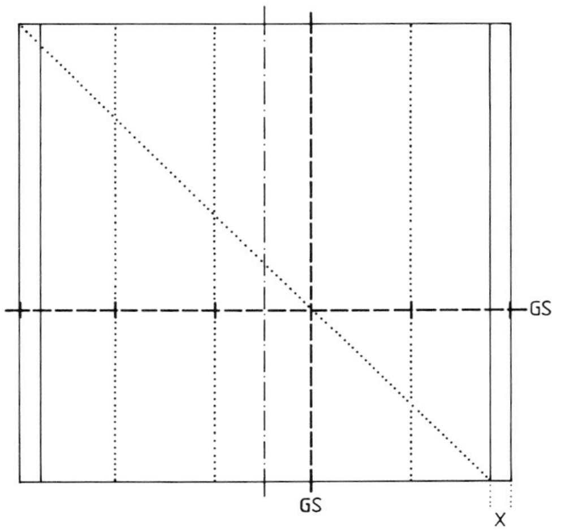

149

Fig. 112

Fig. 113

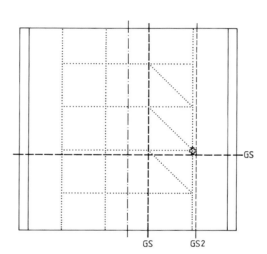

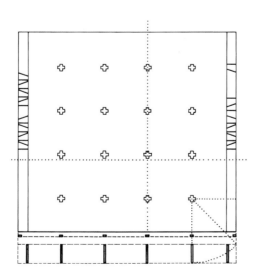

Fig. 114

Fig. 110–114 Ground plan analysis of the Govenor's Palace

Open Hand Monument
Martyrs' Memorial
Tower of the Shadows
Pyramid
1951/1985   Chandigarh   India

Jane Drew, Le Corbusier's project architect in Chandigarh, is said to have inspired him to place symbolic monuments on the great plateau.[81] As Le Corbusier liked talking about himself in the third person, this could certainly be a projection and in fact his own wishes were being expressed indirectly. He had for a long time been interested in the symbolism of signs, and his sketchbooks are overflowing with them. The first hand was published in the Modulor in 1948 and regularly appeared in sketch form.

Fig. 115   Work did not start on the Open Hand Monument until the early eighties, with contributions from all over the world. It was finally completed in 1985. It is one of several signs designed for the plateau. They are a cross between building and free sculpture. They are of no immediate functional use, but they do have a role in terms of space and architecture. These signs, as buildings or even reliefs – for example drawings for the Modulor, the man with the outstretched arm, the harmonious spiral, changing times of day, the play of the sun, portrayals of nature and the Open Hand – were intended to enrich the plateau, but only a few of them were realized. It is certain that these built signs would have introduced an indispensable scale in-between the large buildings, spaced very far apart, as they would have relativized the distance.

The Open Hand is a figure of an abstract hand, i.e. a hand interpreted artistically, that Le Corbusier refined in various stages. Its middle three fingers make an even vertical formation and the thumbs and little finger are both opening outwards. The lines of the hand and the ball of the thumb are clearly present on the surface as curved notches. The hand is a kind of large flat relief, cast in bronze and mounted on a cylindrical rod. It can turn, which means that the wind comes into play and can change the position of the figure. A box-shaped concrete substructure, closed on three sides and open to the plateau, forms the "plinth" of the monument, although it is in fact more like a frame. This frame links the clearly visible sign at the top with a lower space, a trough, containing tiers of seating and a lectern in a place of assembly. This place was set lower as part of the modulation of the site, also with the intention of leaving the monument and its substructure entirely visible. A ramp on one side and a flight of steps opposite provide access to the lower level.

Assemblies in the open air as part of the process of ju-

risdiction suggest the ancient world, and thus this architecture is reminiscent of a mixture of a prehistoric site and Greek theatre. Unfortunately it was never used for its prescribed function.

The Open Hand is probably intended as a sign of exhortation, but its critics[82] find it essentially kitschy, a far cry from an appropriate symbolizing force for a rather soberly conceived town like Chandigarh, whose rational plan and meaningless "centre" do not provide any reference point for complex interpretation. Von Moos[83] suggests that it embodies casual giving and receiving, as an allegory of a gesture that is both active and passive: drawing the powers of life while consciously subordinated to the laws of the universe. And Le Corbusier

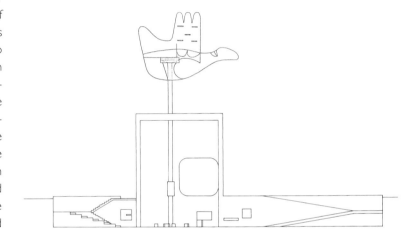

Fig. 115 Elevation of the Open Hand monument
(redrawn after Le Corbusier by Klaus-Peter Gast, 1999)

himself says: "... a plastic gesture charged with a profoundly human content. A symbol very appropriate to the new situation of a liberated and independent earth. A gesture which appeals to a fraternal collaboration and solidarity between all men and all nations of the world. Also a sculptural gesture ... capable of capturing the sky and engaging the earth."[84]

It must be noted critically that sculptures as Western and abstract symbols were alien to the culture of the country at the time, even though Le Corbusier likes to emphasize the popular character of his drawings and that the Indian architects Doshi and Varma, as Le Corbusier's fellow planners in Chandigarh, like interpreting the symbolism of the Open Hand and consider it to be correct and appropriate. The general public in Chandigarh will certainly not have been interested in walking about and appreciating the finer points of the Capitol buildings and its signs, especially as the government quarter is some distance away. The only way in which this desire, frequently formulated in the drawings in

---

[81] Sounding slightly anecdotal: "One evening on the lawn outside the Rest-House of Chandigarh, where Jane Drew, Pierre Jeanneret, Maxwell Fry and Le Corbusier have their base, Jane Drew said: 'Le Corbusier, you should set up in the heart of the Capitol the signs which symbolize the basis of your philosophy and by which you arrived at your understanding of the art of city design. These signs should be known – they are the key to the creation of Chandigarh'", from: Boesiger/Girsberger (ed.), "Le Corbusier 1910–65", p. 229.

[82] For example Curtis, "Le Corbusier, Ideas and Forms", p. 200.
[83] Von Moos, "Le Corbusier", p. 358.
[84] Quoted from Curtis, "Le Corbusier, Ideas and Forms", p. 199.

The revolving monument with its substructure and open assembly area

The Open Hand monument at a distance from Parliament Building and Secretariat

The sunken sitting area for assemblies

particular, for a plaza used actively by the townspeople could be fulfilled would have been to place the government buildings in the town centre, perhaps in the culminating figure of an area for mixed use. But Le Corbusier never even looked at this idea: the Capitol, a work of art, placed in isolation and not to be sullied by secular buildings was an integrated creation that dominated his thinking. Thus the sculptural signs are a direct illustration of his desire for autonomous artistic work. They echo the idea of unblemished creation and personal – and thus for Le Corbusier "correct" – expressive force. He overlooked the fact that this only increased the gulf between the secular urban structure and the work of art.

The Open Hand is a work on the Capitol site that is undoubtedly necessary within the composition as a whole. It seems important, and makes a contribution to formulating the lines and borders of the plateau more clearly. But like all the other Capitol buildings, this structure is isolated and remains a lonely presence, not just because some of the structures are missing but especially because of the unintended waste land between the buildings, which is like a wilderness turned into steppe.

The following geometrical analysis will look at the composition of the view, at the elevation for once, and not the ground plan, as this approach will be more productive. Here too plan analysis is definitely rewarding. As the first example in this book, the Villa Schwob, has already shown, Le Corbusier ties the ground plan and the elevation into the geometrical structure to exactly the same extent.

"Assembly pit" in front of Parliament Building and Secretariat

Open Hand, Martyrs' Memorial, High Court, Tower of the Shadows and Pyramid, view from the Parliament's portico

Fig. 116 A double square of a defined size is the initial figure for the overall plan outline. The distance 2X between the tip of the index finger and the tip of the outstretched thumb is then "pushed in" and the two sections overlap.

Fig. 117 This overall outline is divided in the proportion of the Golden Section (broken bold line). The dividing line GS forms the vertical axis for a new square frame. The half of the overlapping width X is then taken three units (3X) to the left to establish the square. The right-hand trace of the square is established by reflecting across GS. The square forms the outline of the substructure on the entrance level, whose plane is then located in a new line below the double square outline. Projecting the square outline upwards precisely defines the upper edge of the little finger with its upper line, and the upper notches on the two middle fingers. A smaller square can be added below the middle axis of the overlapping double square and extending to the line GS, and this represents the rear opening in the substructure. The line GS is the Open Hand's actual balancing line.

Fig. 116–119 Analysis of the elevation of the Open Hand monument

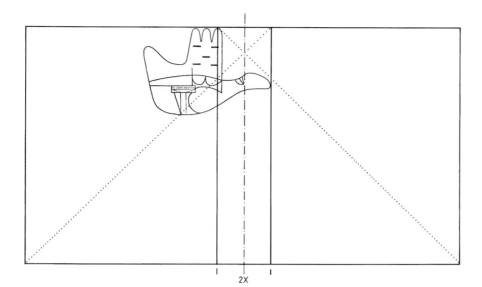

Fig. 116

2X

155

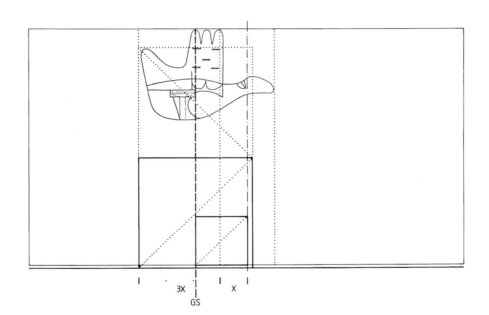

Fig. 117

3X X

GS

Fig. 118   The inner edges of the substructure can now be defined. The distance from the centre line of the double square to the left-hand outer line of the substructure is again divided in the proportion of the Golden Section (GS2). Thus the left-hand edge of the round column with a revolving top is established. Its width is equivalent to the width of the sides of the substructure. Other Golden Section proportions confirm the links described. The area proportion of the Golden Section *maior* (bold broken long diagonal) can be established on the basis of the overall width of the substructure. The upper line of this area meets the plinth-like end point at the top of the column, and its extension on the right precisely meets the extreme tip of the thumb.

Fig. 119   It now becomes clear that the width of the overlapping double square defines the overall width of the complex including its sunken section. Its depth is determined by a simple square dimension that can be added on the basis of the horizontal line developed in fig. 118 and the extension of the right-hand outer line of the substructure. The diagonal of this square defines the depth of the sunken area at its point of intersection with the left-hand outside line of the overall figure.

156

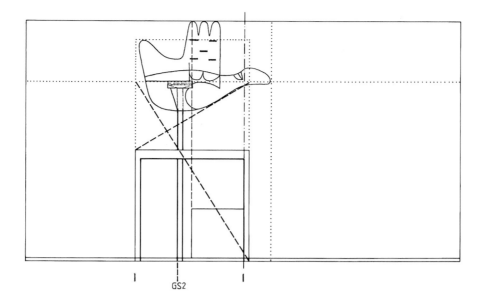

Fig. 118

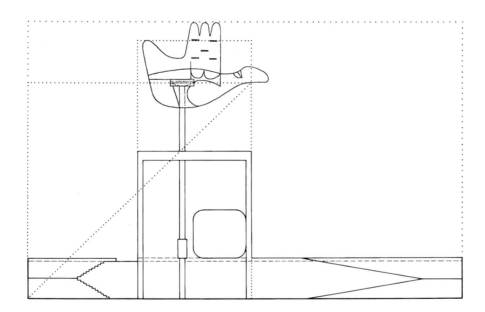

Fig. 119

There are other symbolic buildings in the centre of the complete Capitol complex. They include the Martyrs' Memorial as a monument to the victims of the division of the state. It consists of a long ramped structure surrounding a courtyard, and concludes in another shorter ramp. The Memorial is situated on the edge of a narrow part of the plateau between the Parliament Building and the High Court, before the lower area for the long access road to the planned Governor's Palace. Opposite it is a long plinth-like protrusion framing a lower courtyard. This was intended to give access to a truncated pyramid, an artificial mound of earth, planned to be enclosed by concrete walls at the sides. Unfortunately neither this entrance as an exterior complex nor the pyramid itself were realized completely. Its surface was intended to have an abstract representation of the path taken by the sun in a whole day engraved on it in concrete, but the last and most important part was not built. Today this section is covered by a green area that has been trodden bare by people looking for a good viewing point. The pyramid as a building type and its surface symbolism are clear indications to a transcendental reference to sphere and cosmos, of which there are also echoes in the Capitol buildings.

Another building in this context is the Tower of the Shadows opposite the Martyrs' Memorial: this is a square pavilion relating exactly to the points of the compass. Its walls are made up exclusively of horizontal slabs between which brise-soleil of various sizes were added. A square in the proportion 1 to root 2 minor was arranged diagonally on its roof, providing additional daylight for the interior via brise-soleil. Orientation to the points of the compass suggests the most precise rendering of the light and shade effects caused by the path of the sun at various times of the year – and the pavilion is thus an instrument for measuring time and light.

From this pavilion a large ramp leads out to the sunken entrance level of the pyramid. Thus this magical and mystical structure provides access to the pyramid and, in connection with the highly symbolic value of the pyramid in particular as a sun reflector of Egyptian origin is reminiscent of the Jantar Mantar cosmological measuring instruments in the Indian cities of Delhi and Jaipur from the 18th century. It confirms the assumed cosmological aspect of the whole Capitol site.

Short access ramp to the Martyrs' Memorial

Plateau with Martyrs' Memorial on the left and pavilion right and the High Court in the background

View of the pyramid from the inside the pavilion

The Tower of the Shadows pavilion on the edge of the overgrown plateau

Distortion of the brise-soleil walls of the pavilion

Detail of the brise-soleil walls

Façade detail

Open side of the pavilion facing the Parliament Building

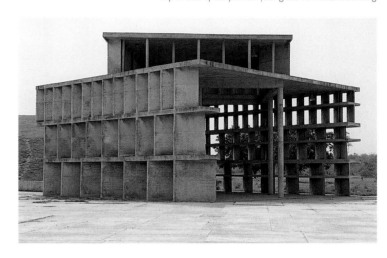

Pavilion with Secretariat in the background

Pavilion ramp in front of the Parliament Building portico

Villa Shodan
1951–1956   Ahmedabad   India

While working on Chandigarh, Le Corbusier also prepared several designs for the northern Indian town of
Ahmedabad, including three private houses. The first
client dropped out after a short time, but Le Corbusier
was able to carry on with the other two designs. Then
the second client Surottam Hutheesing finally sold his
house to a friend, Shyamubhai Shodan, who took it over
without further alterations and built it without objections – though on another site. Both clients were textile manufacturers, and so knew each other. Le Corbusier had already met them during his first visits to
India through the contract for their Millowners' Association Building, which is described below. Hutheesing
was a wealthy young bachelor with an ambitious private life. The architecture of what became the Shodan
villa in particular should be seen in this light, as the design was tailored to his personal needs. Although
Shodan had a different life-style he took over the architecture and thus to a certain extent the attitude to life
that it expressed. However, it is not possible to say to

what extent this individual architecture influenced his
personal behaviour.

Le Corbusier used the idea of an umbrella roof for this
design. The function of providing protection from sun
and rain that is so urgently needed in India is transferred directly to a new architectural element in residential building. This roof detaches itself completely
from the building underneath in visual terms, but unlike
the roof of the High Court in the Capitol in Chandigarh
it is not an independent form in its own right. It precisely maintains the outline of the building as a "raised"
roof slab. Its right-angled, reduced form is part of the
volume and forms an integral element of the overall
outline. This invokes the contradictory impression of a
detached building section that is still part of the body
of the building. In earlier phases of the design the roof
was in part still a direct component of the external outline; it was either fused with the outer wall or stretched
completely freely above it as a segmental arch structure. The arch idea could be linked with the Parliament
Building and the High Court in Chandigarh. These were
planned at the same time and were intended to have
arches from the outset.

The overall concept was fixed as early as 1952. Doshi,
who also worked on the Capitol in Chandigarh, was an
important colleague ultimately responsible for working

View of the drive to the main entrance

162

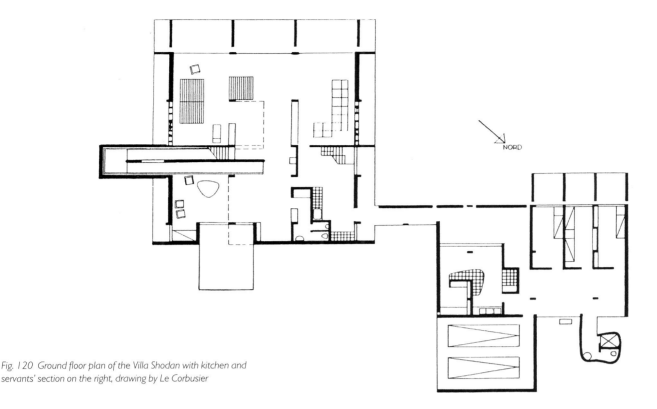

Fig. 120 Ground floor plan of the Villa Shodan with kitchen and servants' section on the right, drawing by Le Corbusier

out the plans. He was later the key intermediary in realizing another important piece of architecture in Ahmedabad, Kahn's Indian Institute of Management. Ahmedabad became the only city in the world to have buildings by Le Corbusier and Kahn.

Fig. 120 A striking feature of the ground floor plan of the Villa Shodan is that it is divided into a main building and a single-storey side building containing the kitchen, garage and servants' rooms. The main building has five storeys in all, in which Le Corbusier develops complex vertical and horizontal spatial layers. The approximately square plan contains the entrance salon on ground level, which is divided from the two-storey, south-west facing main living-room behind by a lateral ramp structure that thrusts outwards to the left. Unlike the Villa Savoye, in which the ramp is a feature that *guides* anyone coming in, indeed almost demands motion, the ramp here is a sculpturally independent structure that *diverts* movement. It practically blocks the way – as in the High Court – and forces people to change direction, and is thus a dividing rather than a connecting element. Next to it are the dining area and a multi-purpose room somewhere between kitchen and dining-room. A striking feature of the ground plan is its right-angled quality, with only a freely rounded sanitary figure as a contrast on the side building. In the upper storeys – not shown here – free formal design is restricted to a few walls of sanitary areas. The crucial feature now is the way in which levels are interlinked by overlapping spatial lay-

ers, which again come close to the Rowe/Slutzky Transparency concept to which we have already referred (Villa Savoye, High Court). Multiply staggered areas linked by air-spaces are shaped, that penetrate each other inside the firmly defined outer lines of the building, *without cancelling each other out*. This creates a very varied interplay of internal galleries and external terraces, climaxing in an uppermost "viewing platform" in the form of a level immediately below the roof that can be reached only via a walkway. This could have been meant to express the client's casual and light-hearted life-style, but Le Corbusier was more interested in an opportunity to realize spaces that were linked in a complex way. Three different spatial areas are staggered one above the other. Their volumes and sophisticated colour schemes are reminiscent of early De Stijl concepts, as Serenyi[85] points out.

The floating umbrella roof is supported by a load-bearing system of slab-like pillars that are continued down to the ground floor and merge into dividing walls there. They form a structure that determines the ground plan to an extent as – like the column system in the Governor's Palace – they are intended to visibly separate load-bearing and covering functions. But in the Villa Shodan the outside walls are also used to disperse forces, so that this concept that was so lucid earlier is blurred here. Also the ground floor plan is not as sophisticated as the innovative solutions devised for the twenties villas, and it seems as though the influential

85 Serenyi, "Timeless but of its Time…".

hand of another designer is making its presence felt. Thus the remark that *"... the Shodan Villa recalls the ingenuity of the Villa Savoye in a tropical setting"*[86] is scarcely the point, because there are no similarities except for the fact that a ramp is used here as well. The ramp in the Shodan Villa is reduced to the status of a formal element; its function as a central link between the planes of a richly experienced spatial interchange with a sense of "joyful" movement – as in the Villa Savoye – is scarcely credible here. The terraces and airspaces on the upper floors are more eventful, but the somewhat inept way in which they are connected by narrow walkways is more like "climbing up" than a means of access that has been carefully thought through. The undoubtedly attractive changes of space within this cavity between the umbrella roof and the body of the building are staged: as a theatrical venue for parties and ceremonies, which invites "residential activity", or at least that one should walk about on the architecture. A "hole" in the roof even includes the varied plane of the sky in the architecture, so that the contradiction between acting as protection and at the same time as a link creates a tension reaching across the gap. Perforating sections of the building, walls and ceilings (cut-out window in the solarium of the Villa Savoye, crosswalls in the portico of the Assembly Building, ramp walls in the High Court) is a constant theme in Le Corbusier's architecture, opening up intended or chance views and making various layers of things "behind" visible.

As in other buildings in India, Le Corbusier uses his brise-soleil to filter the sunlight; they are really wall slabs placed in front of the façade, and here they end up as a cubic composition. They are almost detached from the actual building by a partition line and linked at the longitudinal wall only at a kind of "predetermined breaking point", the "wall" made up of vertical and horizontal sheets creates its own spaces in front of the glass plane of the façade because of the effect of depth they give. The individual parts fuse on the surface into a continuous outline, creating a body that binds everything into it. Closed as well as open spaces of different sizes are concealed behind this brise-soleil wall, creating different spacing for the vertical elements, which retain a certain degree of autonomy. The artful interplay of spaces staggered one behind the other, sometimes to great depths, is particularly clear in the front view. Here we see Le Corbusier's intention to make changing levels that are the brise-soleil wall, the façade of the building, the volumes behind and even the rear wall of the whole building visible to the same degree. The vivid colour schemes of the façade parts further enliven the layering of the levels. As we are largely not dealing with levels containing glass here, in other words transparent walls, it is not possible to see how the internal spaces overlap from the outside. The south-west façade in particular is reminiscent of Le Corbusier's purist pictorial compositions in the twenties, in which clearly defined objects are stacked one behind the other and sometimes overlap and penetrate each other. Coloured areas and sets of lines make an effect something like Mondrian, but are now additionally shifted in the third dimension. One new feature are the sculpturally rounded "window eyes" in the essentially closed long walls, borrowed from the famous wall in the chapel at Ronchamp, which was created at the same time. The "eyes" combine with glass in rectangular frames to make carefully proportioned perforated walls. In contrast with the façade which opens on to the garden, the entrance side presents itself as a closed, rough concrete wall with, however, an inviting entrance umbrella. The architecture of the Villa Shodan does not make an amiable impression either. Like the Capitol buildings it consists of concrete with the shuttering marks visible, whose coarse structure is further heightened with coloured paint. But it is very much in harmony with the Indian climate and the positive view of this culture of vivid colour.

[86] Boesiger/Girsberger (ed.), "Le Corbusier 1910–65", p. 86.

View of the main entrance from the drive

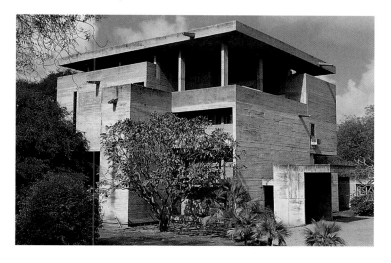

Entrance detail from drive

Façade detail with prodtruding volume of ramp

Corner detail with upper terrace floor

Façade detail with surface showing shuttering marks

Detail of the loggia on the upper floor

Brise-soleil on the south-west side

Garden façade

View from the west

View with brise-soleil and the staggered upper storey terraces

The following is an analysis of the ground plan of the main part of the building (excluding the kitchen wing) to establish its geometrical structure.

Fig. 121   A square of defined size is the starting point for the design. Once more it is the predefined "proposition" as the start of the design, a point of transition between a rational and an irrational process.

Fig. 122   The square (dotted diagonal) is shifted by a dimension X in a horizontal direction. Together the starting and final positions form a new rectangle. This produces the horizontal axis Y and the vertical axis of the shifted square Z2.

Fig. 123   A quarter of the shifted square (closely dotted line) is extended by the proportion of the Golden Section. The field of this area proportion (bold broken line) overlaps with the quarter square in such a way that two peripheral zones are created at the top and the bottom. The upper peripheral zone – as an extension of the shifted square – overlaps with the quarter square by a trace width of defined size. This trace establishes the distance of the brise-soleil wall from the body of the building. The upper new outside line represents the limits of the brise-soleil. Below the original horizontal axis Y, the lower peripheral zone defines the width of the ramp, which thrusts out considerably. Z is now the vertical central axis of the rectangle.

Fig. 121–125 Ground plan analysis of the Villa Shodan

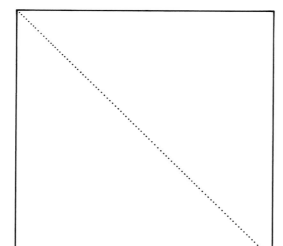

Fig. 121

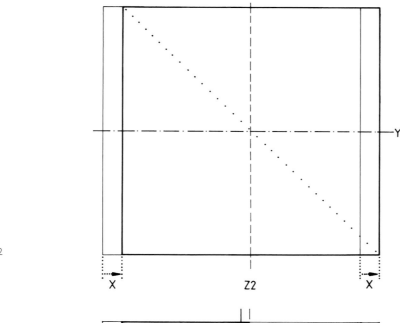

Fig. 122

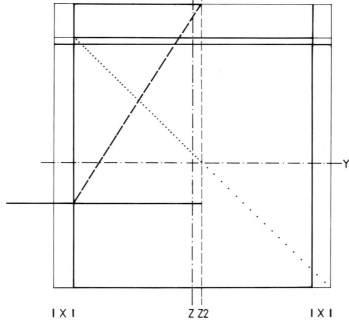

Fig. 123

Fig. 124 The distance proportion of the Golden Section (GS) is established from the width of the shifted starting square. The area proportion of this division of the square and other areas of the same proportion can also be illustrated (bold broken diagonals).

This vertical trace GS is reflected over the central axis Z. Both traces form the central axis of the wall slabs of the brise-soleil façades.

Walls of a defined size can now be added on the inner traces of the shifted width. They form the enclosing line for the main building on the ground floor while the protruding volume of the upper floors indicates the outer lines. Wall slabs as brise-soleil elements are also arranged in the extension of the outside walls.

Fig. 125 The supports are arranged in the form of narrow slabs on the Golden Section division traces. Their spacing is based on the one hand on the halving W of the distance of the upper line of the main building from the line of the ramp and on the other hand on the width of the ramp. This produces the distance B from the lower line of the ramp on the left, which then leads – added at W – to the lowest row of columns. Here the entrance is placed, with its inlet, which is the size of the distance between the columns and the outer wall.

The ramp is clearly limited by Y and Z. Its length, and that of the entrance roof, can be tied into a new enclosing square.

The Villa Shodan is different from Le Corbusier's other buildings. It is not typical of his work in terms of a surprisingly uncomplicated, less than virtuoso plan design, for example the essentially "disfunctional" ramp, placed so that it makes next to no sense, a conventional ground floor and complex encapsulations on the upper floors with difficult access. The geometrical structure of this architecture does not seem complex either, but wooden, and thus suggests a hand other than Le Corbusier's. But it is felt that the master's work can be clearly sensed in the façades, the composition of the brise-soleil and the tension-filled body of the building as a whole. Perhaps this is in fact the principal contribution that he made.

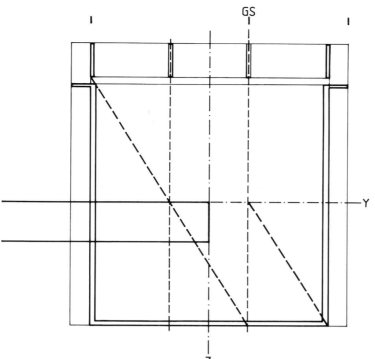

Fig. 124

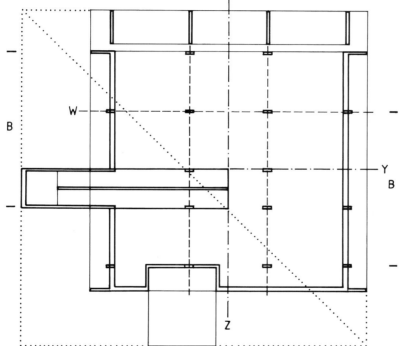

Fig. 125

Millowners' Association Building
1951–1954   Ahmedabad   India

Le Corbusier acquired five commissions in all in the northern city of Ahmedabad after his first visit to India in 1951. They are all associated with a family clan with whom Le Corbusier made immediate contact, as important members of it held influential positions in politics and commerce. The clients were some of the city's textile manufacturers, the so-called Millowners, who had formed an association some time before. They mainly belonged to a Hindu sub-group, the Jains, a community that lived their lives according to strict rules and were successful in business.

Le Corbusier's commissions included a culture centre (built: a museum), three private houses, of which two were built, and finally the Millowners' Association Build-

ing, a new building for the textile manufacturers' offices and meetings. Planning started under their director Hutheesing, a young and well-to-do Jain. Hutheesing also commissioned a house for himself. The plans for this were finally sold to another member, Shodan, as has already been mentioned.

The Millowners' Building takes up an old Le Corbusier theme as its basic concept. It consists of a block-like building open only on two opposite sides. Both ends acquire sculpturally shaped concrete façades through brise-soleil structures, with the long sides presenting almost completely closed brick walls. As the brise-soleil walls extend over the full width of the façade they seem so dominant that the actual "body of the building" disappears behind them. The brise-soleil turn out as independent figures with a physical presence placed in front of the building, both on the entrance side and also on the rear façade, facing the river. They are no longer part of the flow of the building's lines, as they were in the Parliament Building in Chandigarh, but remain indepen-

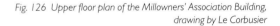

Fig. 126 Upper floor plan of the Millowners' Association Building, drawing by Le Corbusier

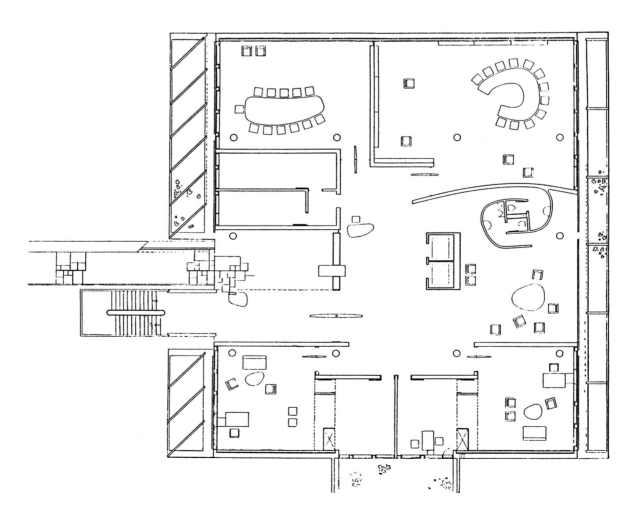

Detail of the main front with staircase, ramp and brise-soleil

dent. Only on the brick sides are these façade sections linked by concrete lintels running the whole way round. On the entrance side – facing west – the façade is dominated by diagonally placed brise-soleil, whose outermost lines fuse with the horizontal levels, as in Chandigarh, but on the rear, eastern side there are free-standing walls running at right angles as a kind of grille. This design shows the emergence of the completely autonomous and detached façade form, which in the case of the Shodan Villa still merges with the body of the building at the sides and can now be varied and used for any other building.

Fig. 126   The building programme was not very extensive, and is very difficult to grasp clearly. It is intended to provide offices on the ground floor, along with a foyer with access to a separate room providing food and drink. Above this were the management rooms and offices, with access principally via the ramp, which thrust out for some distance. There was to be a two-storey meeting-room with a lavish foyer and gallery access to the roof terrace on the top floor. The ramp and the terrace next to it provided the dominant sculptural elements of the entrance façade including the ramp, the stairs next to it and a lift-shaft section opposite them inside. The relatively large volume with little usable floor space arises from the extremely generous treatment of access and lounge facilities on all levels. Here the view through to the adjacent wide river with the old town

opposite is important as an attractive reference point. The building opens in response to the direction of movement towards the river and the activities that take place there. As the two lower floors are used for offices, the façades are largely glazed, thus producing an overlapping structure of coloured glass frames and brise-soleil walls similar to that of the Villa Shodan. The zoning – closed at the bottom and largely open at the top – is also like that of the Villa Shodan and even further enhanced here: foyer zones and the entrance side have spaces that are completely open, so that the dramatic quality of the "inserted" curved bodies of the sanitary areas and the hall is particularly well developed. Le Corbusier plans these "empty spaces" as zones where people can be together, in which public and private functions can meet, for celebrations and to symbolize the way in which the clan sticks together, or also to experience the architecture itself while moving. And Le Corbusier also had a completely new free hand in terms of design here to the extent that this is a building without any actual conclusion to the rooms. Thus he did not produce a building in the traditional sense, but rather an open *covering body*, into which other covering bodies were placed. This covering of zones as an act of individual limitation is emphasized by the transparent quality of the façades, especially at the back, with the interior areas of the building being put on show.

But this approach of clear demarcation and juxtaposition of an orthogonal structure on the outside and rounded figures inside provides no scope for spatial overlapping. Complex spatial relationships like those in the design for the Villa Stein, in which layers of space belonging to different areas penetrate each other and are staggered behind each other, are not conceivable on this basis. Here every volume is isolated and says: "I am an individual", it remains an entity in its own right, and is thus readily intelligible. It is not possible for an ambiguous, encoded spatial continuum to emerge and express itself in this way. And the formal contrast between an orthogonal frame and curved free forms, which cropped up very early in Le Corbusier's work, seems rather too direct in the interior, almost superficial, and carelessly designed. Here the free forms emerge from the spontaneous idea, they were not refined or devised by geometrical calculation, and so remain in a

View of the Millowners' Association Building from the main drive

kind of natal condition. Thus a subjective formal canon without universal relevance is created, rather like many of the minor figures in the Capitol in Chandigarh. It is noticeable that the rounded forms seem to writhe, because the walls draw in on themselves like "shrunken" rooms that used to be much larger. This suggests movement, and is certainly the most important contrast between the essentially rigid framework of the brise-soleil in front and the structurally necessary round columns. The dynamic element of this contrast is developed more strongly here than in Shodan, but one has to wonder whether this drama has not become unduly "interesting". The interplay of contrasting forms presented here seems to be straining for effect and shows a lack of subtlety. There is no longer any intention of co-ordinating within a refined composition, but just a rather coarse contrast. No coming together to form

complex spaces, or even spaces in between is intended, but just an unambiguous here and there. The foyer and the other circulation areas outside the curved bodies can thus be suspected of being "left over", after the individual showpieces have been staged.

But when entering the assembly room you are in fact not only impressed by the free curves, but also by Le Corbusier's virtuosity with the interplay of asymmetrical wall formations without a single right angle, the skylight that inclines downwards towards the centre and the diagonal run of the wall cladding. Vertiginous dynamics suddenly impinge, and you think you are entering another world. Le Corbusier chose the shape of the roof-top structure from the Governor's Palace in the Capitol in Chandigarh for the skylight, and here it directs light from the sky into the room by sweeping diagonally up on both sides. This skylight is also an independent figure, which Le Corbusier is able to use almost interchangeably elsewhere as a "form as such". The roof terrace, following an ideal of the twenties, was not only intended to be a viewing platform, and a visual representation of cooling for the room, along with the skylight figure. It was intended to be a space that could be used and enjoyed directly. Le Corbusier's efforts to ensure that users of the building enjoy being in it and are able to relax and enjoy the architecture can be sensed not only in the foyer areas with their view, the bars and seating facilities, but also in this roof area. The building is in a dilapidated state at the time of writing, the family clan of Millowners has fallen apart, the textile business has gone into decline. The impressive hall is used only as a storeroom and book depository, the roof garden is in ruins and the exquisite forms have acquired a patina of dirt and rust. It remains to be seen and to be hoped whether the building, which is certainly suitable for other uses, can have new life breathed into it as an important cultural monument in Ahmedabad.

Detail of the entrance side with the staircase protruding as a sculptural feature

Detail of the back of the building with open zones on the upper floors

Access ramp for the first floor level

Detail of the brise-soleil on the front façade

Upper floor with hall skylight

Ground floor access area

Foyer with stairs to the top floor

Foyer on the upper hall floor

Upper floor access area

Perspective on Late Works in Europe: Chapel of Notre-Dame-du-Haut Monastery of La Tourette

Le Corbusier's most important late works in Europe came into being at the same time as the buildings in India. These include the designs for the chapel in Ronchamp (1950–1954) and the extension for the monastery in Eveux-sur-Arbresle near Lyon (1953–1961), which have become icons of 20th century architecture. It is revealing to compare these two works, which are now acknowledged to be classical and thus "timeless", with the buildings produced in the Indian context. They can also represent other important buildings in this phase. Ronchamp and La Tourette are not too far apart in terms of date, and it is possible to establish a parallel between them and the Indian buildings with their long period of gestation from 1952. They complete the picture of the late work that has been developed from a particular point of view here.

Planning for the chapel started in 1950, and produced a structure that astonished the architectural world. Critics acknowledged the quality of the building, but thought that Le Corbusier had betrayed the language he had established for himself, which had so far been based largely on the right angle. In fact the building is unique, not just in terms of Le Corbusier's work, but within the whole of twentieth century architecture. Le Corbusier creates a space that is asymmetrical in all its dimensions, enclosed on three sides by double, non-parallel walls – a complete novelty in comparison with his previous work, or so it would seem. These walls contain *rooms*: on the main entrance side they are "light rooms", window zones that widen towards the inside, and on the other side prayer niches and a side-room. On the south side there are a few pews on the floor, which slopes towards the east-facing altar. The curved roof covers an exterior space that uses the open air as an outdoor chapel.

Fig. 127

Bird's-eye view of the Chapel of Ronchamp

The building does not have any "sides" that can be pinned down unambiguously, as fluent transitions lead to surprising relationships between sections of the building and of the walls. This means that they can be defined in a constantly changing way, with the result that the viewer is drawn compulsively around the building. The ground plan shows that no part of the building is based on right angles. Instead of this, the dominant feature is the curved walls of the prayer niches, which are held in a state of tension, a key motif of this period in the work of Le Corbusier, and one that has often been described before. The bracket-like figure of a buckled wall, often with different radii, can also be found in the roof of the Parliament portico and, opened out widely, on the roof of the Governor's Palace in Chandigarh, in the curved ground plan figures of the Millowners' Building, in Le Corbusier's lamp designs, in the "Modulor Man's" hand the chapel gargoyles – a sign, or perhaps just one of Le Corbusier's favourite motifs, based on previously existing, transformed models from nature. Other parallels with the Indian buildings, which came soon after in terms of time, are the curves of the roof figure both inside and outside, and also asymmetrical wall figures. These curves can be seen, for example, in the hall lighting in the Millowners' Building, the Parliament portico and the vaults of the High Court. And the chapel's solid and weighty element, contradicted in places by a screen-like, thin-skinned form, can also be found in the Indian buildings.

Ronchamp is an image that helped to shape the Indian designs in many ways. A mystical link can also be produced at points where interior and exterior are dynamic, fluent. The sense of opening up to the sphere in Chandigarh, a transcendental reference, is prepared very subtly in Ronchamp, in a variety of ways. The formal symbolism associated with this, and also the metaphysics of light in the chapel, must have had a considerable influence on the Capitol buildings, their sign world, or even on the overall disposition. As described above, the Capitol site is to be understood as intended to provide a metaphysical field for making contact with things that lie outside our direct horizon of perception – if only figuratively.

179

Fig. 127 Ground plan of the Chapel of Ronchamp

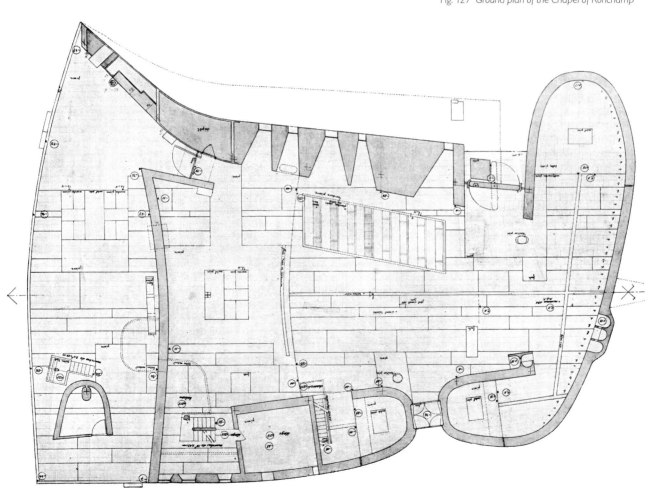

Outdoor altar and lighting towers in the background

There may be an impression that this structure was created quite spontaneously and intuitively, and that there was nothing "rational" behind it, possibly because of its spiritual character or precisely because of the design principle. But there is something that makes it quite clear that Le Corbusier – as in all his other buildings – used rational principles when designing the Ronchamp chapel, placing them in an ambiguous relationship of tension with subjective propositions. The floor structure is a cement slab covering determined by Modulor dimensions – and thus by the Golden Section –, and it was laid entirely on the basis of right angles. Equally, a exterior campanile that was part of the original plan but never realized would have been a steel framework with a square grid structure that gives a further hint of an "ordering principle" at work. Le Corbusier himself says in his own publications[87] that Modulor dimensions were used in the chapel, but does not give a concrete reference point. So floor structure and campanile show that there was a rational system, but admittedly it is scarcely decipherable because of the complex wall figures. Perhaps there is a rational key here that holds the disposition of the curved wall figures "in place". One idea that suggests itself is that the careful composition of the "perforated" south façade, the ratios of the

View with outdoor altar and main access side on the left

---

[87] For example in Boesiger/Girsberger (ed.), "Le Corbusier 1910–65", p. 259.

lengths of the parts of the building to their height and width and the position of the accents were not chosen on a basis of mere sensibility, but this could only be confirmed by detailed measurement of the building as a basis for concrete statements about proportional dependency.

The motif of curved walls arranged within a right-angled frame, varied and developed further from the time of the Villa Besnus, acquires a new dimension in Ronchamp. The walls, which are free but oscillate in a state of tension have left this frame here, they have ex-*ploded* it, and thus emancipated themselves. The curved lines dominate now. They no longer represent internal, interesting contrasting figures, but make up the body of the building *themselves*, and act out their part on an orthogonal plateau, in other words they "move" on the given floor area as an ordering pattern. This is clear not least from the dynamic inherent in the plan: in the breaking open of the solid, broad wall as an act of distortion, in the slits, holes and perforations that do not merely express some mystic quality of light, and in the outward-thrusting curves. The rounded "subsidiary forms" of earlier ground plan concepts now play the main part as self-confident and independent figures. Does this mean that Le Corbusier as a personality has

now won his fight to be independent, to express his individuality, to express *himself*? Was the beloved shackle of rational calculation more of a hindrance than a help? But in the history of architecture the great struggle between subject and object as a source of constant mental anguish often led to the most outstanding creations. Le Corbusier continued to understand this, as the designs for his subsequent work show.

This process of dynamic evolution, these "growing" forms, meant that critics classified the chapel as an organic creation. Stirling[88] interpreted this as the building courting popularity to a comparatively larger extent, and thus suggesting that Le Corbusier was turning more markedly to his "public". This assessment fails to take the characteristics of the building design described above into account. Carefully calculated geometry and proportional relations remain perceptible, not just as pose struck by the genius but as a deliberate act of creation. They provide an invisible foothold for an act of free creation and help to make Ronchamp a product of timeless quality, despite its passionate subjectivity. Even today the sight of this building attracts immediate attention and is a source of astonishment – even though pictures of it have often been published in the press and it has been discussed in great detail –,

Rear entrance side with gargoyle on the right

[88] James Stirling, "Ronchamp: Le Corbusier's Chapel and the Crisis of Rationalism", The Architectural Review, March 1956, pp. 144–61.

so that there is no risk of "visual exhaustion" in the case of the Ronchamp chapel. The eye still discovers new and unfamiliar elements, the formal world does not seem exhausted or even modish. We do not ask: why this solid wall, why these curves and diagonals, why the vaulting and cut-off roof with its powerful weight. A number of inadequate interpretations have been provided for all this, but it is difficult to isolate the timeless element and to put it in a nutshell. As von Moos[89] explains, things that are fundamentally rational can no longer be isolated from the irrational, as happened in earlier days. There is no longer a strict either-or, and the Ronchamp chapel is a clear demonstration of this. And so perhaps its represents a new and hybrid architectural type, in which the irrational – apparently the dominant principle here – and the latently irrational are balanced in a wonderful and inexplicable way.

Fig. 128   The design for the monastery building near Lyon was started in May 1953, a year after the Dominicans approached Le Corbusier. It was consecrated in 1961. The U-shaped, block-like building on a very steep slope, with the church added a certain distance away from the side that was actually open, contains the monks'

182

cells and all the other facilities needed by a monastery. The inner courtyard produced by the arrangement of the building contains a symbolically raised access system to all sections of the building with the entrance hall as cloister.

After going through the entrance frame in the Modulor dimensions of 2.26 × 2.26 m it is immediately clear that in this building everything relates to the proportional relationships of measurements developed by Le Corbusier. The block-like framing of the complex, which has a circular element if the church is included, and the rigidity that this produces, contradicts the lively movement inside. The cloister, and the oratory and sacristy buildings and the entrance hall to the refectory all relate to the whole at right angles, but here a more subtle yet dramatic movement is set in train in the "circulation space". The diagonal floor (similar to the floor sloping down to the altar in Ronchamp) of the ramp-like cloister, different ceiling heights and rapid changes in the line patterns of the floors in combination with the shadowlines of the window divisions create a constantly varying picture while one is moving through the various spaces. Light and shade are projected in all their diver-

Bird's-eye view of the monastery of La Tourette

[89] Von Moos, "Le Corbusier", p. 328.

sity and density as overlapping planes. It is – as we have already seen in Le Corbusier's earlier work – a challenge to move, urging the visitor to walk within the architecture. The solid external frame is destabilized by the flux and change that are generated and by the architect's desire to keep the eye constantly on the move. This up and down and interplay of different sections inside the complex contrasts with the constant quality of the clear static lines outside and thus also represents an old motif, though it is interpreted in a new way here. Here constants can be discovered in the work that have accompanied Le Corbusier's entire output.

The façade as such also draws its life from clear contrasts: the three sides of the monastery building show carefully composed apertures for the monks' cells, "flowing" glass walls for the working and functional zones and the internal corridor for the accommodation, but the church block takes the form of a completely closed prism. The light once more becomes a metaphysical component of the spatial experience, similarly to Ronchamp: it is disturbing because of the diversity of openings available to it in the lively system of internal corridors, and it establishes a musical key of

sensibility by setting up undulating rhythms in the exterior façades, and introduces a mystical quality to the dramatic chiaroscuro of the sanctuary. Here space generates itself as a place of transcendental size and creates a direct experience of spiritual perception. Unlike Ronchamp, the accents of the apertures here become extremely reduced sources of "light material", which flows into the space in a deliberate way. This is probably Le Corbusier's most impressive spatial creation, and it is brought into being in angular frugality and dramatic darkness, archaic and absolute. Subject and object become one.

Le Corbusier's ordering system of the Modulor and the dominant proportion of the Golden Section, which are presented to the visitor in the entrance frame, appears to be evident in every detail: in the overall figure with its outline ratios, the aperture formats, the undulating vertical members of the outside windows, which become a component of the opening, and in the disposition and basic form of the buildings inside with cross, square, pyramid and cylinder. It is the culmination of a spirit obsessed with ordering structures, seeking absolute harmony between man and God. But this har-

183

Fig. 128 Ground plan of the monastery of La Tourette

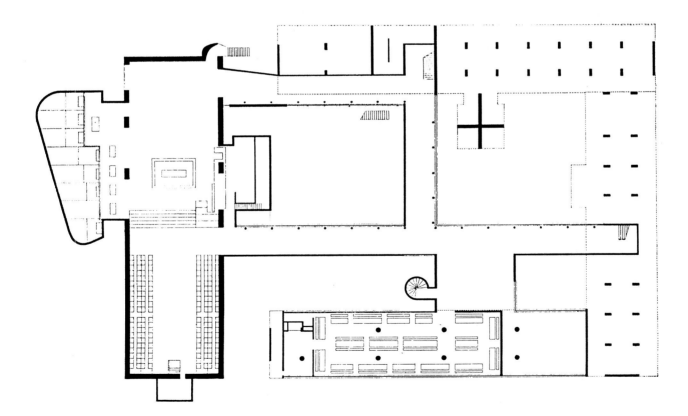

View with the church building on the left

mony appears in the hardest garments. Something that began in 1930 with undressed stone masonry as a contrast with the white cubes that had been completed shortly before, now ends in concrete with a grey patina, rough from the shuttering, notched and unevenly compacted, and almost painfully coarse. *"Everything really new is hard won"*, says Kahn. And the hardness of La Tourette, which appears in parallel form in Chandigarh – but not in the refined chapel of Ronchamp! – is Le Corbusier's expression of an extreme provocation, a hardness full of aggression and relentlessness. His decades-long love affair with concrete is here mixed with the frustration of a professional life including a number of failed designs. The attractive coarseness of the surface of béton brut expresses Le Corbusier's innermost feelings, the sensibility of an artist and the wounded sensitivity of a human being. Something that seems quite natural here, in monastic austerity, became an even coarser, oppressive aestheticism in Chandigarh. It becomes clear at this point that the Capitol in Chandigarh came into being against the background of the two most important buildings in the late work, which challenged Le Corbusier to produce internalized and meditative designs that fitted in with his idea of an otherwordly order. The "magic field" of the Capitol should be judged from this point of view, as its claim to be making transcendental reference seems inappropriate to a certain extent.

View from the south

185

But La Tourette does represent the high point of Le Corbusier's creative work. It is a structure on the interface between limited rational logic, imperfect human inspiration *and* the absolute quality of contemporary geometry as an image of universal creative power.

Cloister in the inner courtyard, roof garden

Dimensions of Rationality in the Work of Le Corbusier

The preceding study of Le Corbusier's work was conducted from a particular point of view. The key feature was not the most comprehensive new documentation possible, but to consider a rational aspect that Le Corbusier himself stressed in various essays and comments. The plan analysis approach made it possible to cast light on this aspect in more detail for the first time and to close a gap in the countless amount of writing on his work. But this should really be a challenge for more examinations of this kind to be produced, as our study can only be a first step towards addressing this particular problem. Measurements of the buildings and surveys of exterior spaces would have to additionally confirm the assertions made, though this seems difficult in the case of the Parliament area in Chandigarh because the dimensions are so enormous. Le Corbusier provided his Modulor system of proportional relations based on the Golden Section, and tried to make architects aware of the importance of rational principles. Selected examples from his complete works have shown how he saw rationality in design and how he applied it, using a systematic analysis of geometrical figurations that form an interdependent system.

As the examples presented have made clear, rationality is present in Le Corbusier's designs in the form of figurative geometry that is usually not immediately perceptible. And yet it is always there, fixing the lines of both façades and ground plans as "concealed images". Their complexity is expressed in an inherent, independent *system* of individual figures, and decoding them leads to an *initial figure*, the beginning of concrete thinking and action. Its structure does not just reveal geometrical links, but in particular reveals the way in which the designer thinks. Plan analysis can comprehensibly illustrate how the intuitively inspired "idea" can be woven into this system, though it has usually been preshaped by patterns of memory, by Le Corbusier's own discoveries, and so by experience. Geometrical figures usually form *frames*, i. e. squares, rectangles or circles that determine the traces of the emerging ground plan, which either exists as realised or is derived from a previous step in the analysis. The geometrical and proportional features discovered in this way are fundamentally dependent on each other and develop the described system successively. In Le Corbusier's case the immense possible number of geometrical links is essentially reduced to two basic figures, though their combinations

in their turn make numerous solutions possible. Starting with the basic figure of the square as the first geometrical proposition and constant, the figure of the Golden Section is frequently generated in the ground plans as an area proportion, another constant that also appears as a mere length proportion in many details of the design. It is striking how much effort Le Corbusier puts into making the essentially rigid geometry of the square dynamic. It is rare to find examples in his work in which the "pure" square is used as the final outline for a ground plan. It is usually set in *motion*. It is distorted by meaningful shifts or overlappings, or becomes a partial figure in the genesis of complex geometry (Citrohan, Savoye, Parliament Building in Chandigarh). Movement often appears in the form of a stretching of the building and its partial figures (long walls with "space slits" and tear-shaped columns in the Villa Stein, outline of the Shodan Villa). The tension thus created is a component of a compositional principle that inclines to movement – and is thus mannerist –, and this is shown particularly in the façades. This procedure can be identified as an important constant in the œuvre, as emphasized movement of geometrical frame figures can be seen throughout Le Corbusier's work. The use of the Golden Section peaks in the "ladder of proportions" developed by Le Corbusier and his colleagues in the Modulor, a system for combining Golden Section proportions as a kind of pattern. Here lies a danger of unthinking schematization, in which the desire for "automatic beauty" is by no means fulfilled, and Le Corbusier was probably subject to the error of thinking that he would always be able to use it to provide the right solution. The movement from the square to the Golden Section proportion can be discerned as early as the design for the Villa Schwob, and it is a determining and dominant constant in the work as a whole. The special feature of the Golden Section area proportion as an infinitely extending spiral of dependent squares (see fig. 74) and the associated "fervent relation" of these two areas explains Le Corbusier's uncommonly great sense of attention and fascination. As can be seen for example in the ground plan of the Citrohan design (see fig. 22), square and Golden Section, linked geometrically, produce an interlaced abundance of areas of the same proportion. The ground plans of the Stein and Savoye villas, but also framing figures for town plans like the one for Saint-Dié contain dominating geometrical figures of these proportions. The anthropometric division of Golden Section relations within a double square generated from a single square in particular can be found again in some designs in the period after the Modulor was developed and became widespread. This figure, which has now become symbolic, even finds its way into the Capitol complex in Chandigarh (see fig. 77). It is only this that makes it possible to understand for the first time Le Corbusier's intention in setting out and introducing a specific "rhythm" into the government quarter. It explains the spacing of the buildings and the dimensions of the plateau-like area.

Another constant in his work is the polarity resulting from moving internal sets of lines within an orthogonal outer frame. In the late work it is possible to see these curved forms being liberated from geometrical calculation, down to the expansion of the curves in Ronchamp, where the rounded walls finally present themselves as outer walls on a ground that is laid out orthogonally. Ronchamp is undoubtedly an extreme part of this series of contrasting wall forms that appeared from the early twenties. Thus this design confirms the continuity of the work, rather than putting it in question. The establishing of hierarchies, the confrontation of contrasts, the modulation of light, the white volumes with perfect lines down to hard, broken béton brut as a scale of surface treatment are all varied facets of virtuoso design that appear in this context.

But plan analysis mainly illuminates the systematic and rational aspect of architecture within the design process. Of course the irrational component is closely linked with the world of evidence that can be analysed. Le Corbusier's architecture is a perfect example of a constant alternation of the two within the genesis of the design, which firstly shapes the creative process in general and secondly the framework of relationships within the particular design.

The rational component that has been worked out here is frequently linked with an inherent irrational element. This fits in with Le Corbusier's conviction that the use of geometry is itself an act that goes beyond rational processes. Basic geometrical forms like square and circle are already charged with meanings by their symbolic character that extend well beyond rational dimensions. For Le Corbusier geometry is the interface with transcendence, the path to metaphysics, the language of the gods. Many of his designs bear the mark of this spiritual aura, though it is never expressly stated. Reshaping the design idea found by intuition, creating carefully calculated sets of lines in this spirit does not just mean that this design approach "stresses reason": above all it produces the quality of a universal language and timeless grandeur. The finding of form that extends from the idea to the first draft takes place on this awareness. Even the roof garden idea in the early designs (formulated in the "Five Points") does not only stress the functional, rational better use of square metres, nor the fresh air. The *relation to the sphere* in the villas, especially Stein and Savoye, extends the architectural space

Le Corbusier

187

into the cosmic dimension, while the attic storey of the Villa Savoye could already be considered a transcendent space. The development of an open storey "right at the top" for making contact with another world continues right up to the very last designs and reaches its climax in the symbolic roof structures on the Parliament Building and the Governor's Palace in the Chandigarh Capitol. The buildings in Ronchamp and Eveux were created in parallel and their spiritual character perfects the transcendental dimension as a preferred subject. The dream and the claim to be architecture that is almost not a part of this world any longer is thus completely met. This culmination places Le Corbusier's work with Louis I. Kahn's as the unsurpassed architecture of the 20th century.

The examination of *order* in Le Corbusier's work draws attention to an aspect rooted in the historical tradition of architecture. Therefore this dimension could easily be misinterpreted as 'no longer up-to-date" in terms of architecture at the beginning of a new millennium. But the material and the results of our study lead to the statement that this very aspect will in fact retain its validity. It would be a misunderstanding to see the analytical system for examining rational principles as a set of instructions for producing high-quality designs automatically. But this approach could stimulate expert readers to embark on critical reflection about their own designs.

Only an attempt to unite order as a product of universal and thus permanently valid relations with individual or subjective intentions can lead to architecture of timeless quality. The aspect that has been addressed and emphasized here definitely contributes to the continuity of 20th century architectural history. Le Corbusier did justice to this claim for continuity with unceasing creative power and the highest possible sensibility concerning the presence of things that are of this world and not of this world.

Selected BIBLIOGRAPHY

Baker, Geoffrey
Le Corbusier, An Analysis of Form, Van Nostrand Reinhold Co. Ltd., New York 1984.

Benton, Timothy J.
Les Villas de Le Corbusier et Pierre Jeanneret 1920–1930, Edition Sers et Fondation Le Corbusier, Paris 1984; English edition: *The Villas of Le Corbusier and Pierre Jeanneret 1920 -1930*, London 1987.

Boesiger, Willy and Girsberger, Hans (ed.) and Stonorov, Oskar (co-editor vol. 1) and Bill, Max (ed. vol. 3)
Le Corbusier und Pierre Jeanneret, Œuvre complète, complete works in 8 volumes: vol. 1: 1910–1929, vol. 2: 1929–1934, vol. 3: 1934–1938, vol. 4: 1938–1946, vol. 5: 1946–1952, vol. 6: 1952–1957, vol. 7: 1957–1965 and vol. 8: The Last Works, Verlag für Architektur Artemis (now Birkhäuser – Publishers for Architecture), Zurich 1965.

Boesiger, Willy and Girsberger, Hans (ed.)
Le Corbusier 1910–65, Verlag für Architektur Artemis (now Birkhäuser – Publishers for Architecture), Zurich 1967.

Brooks, H. Allen (ed.)
The Le Corbusier Archives, the complete drawn work in 33 volumes, Garland International Publishing Inc., New York/London and Fondation Le Corbusier, Paris 1984.

Brooks, H. Allen (ed.)
Le Corbusier, essays by various authors, Princeton University Press, Princeton 1987.

Brooks, H. Allen (ed.)
Le Corbusier 1887–1965, Garland International Publishing Inc., New York 1987.

Brooks, H. Allen
Le Corbusier's Formative Years, The University of Chicago Press, Chicago and London 1997.

Brosmann, Jos (ed.)
Le Corbusier und die Schweiz, Institut für Geschichte und Theorie der Architektur (gta), ETH and Ammann, Zurich 1987.

Choay, Françoise
Le Corbusier, New York 1960.

Colquhoun, Alan
Modernity and the Classical Tradition, Architectural Essays 1980–87, The MIT Press, Cambridge, Mass. 1989 and London 1991.

Curtis, William J. R.
Le Corbusier: Ideas and Forms, Phaidon Press Limited, London 1986.

Curtis, William J. R.
Modern Architecture Since 1900, Phaidon Publishers, London 1982, third edition 1996.

Curtis, William J. R.
Authenticity, Abstraction and the Ancient Sense: Le Corbusier's and Louis Kahn's Ideas of Parliament, in: Perspecta 20, The Yale Architectural Journal, Yale University, New Haven, Rizzoli International Publications Inc., New York 1983.

Denti, Giovanni
*Le Corbusier Bibliografia, Alinea, Milan 1987.

Eisenman, Peter
La Maison Dom-ino and the Self-referential Sign, Oppositions 15/16 (ed. Kenneth Frampton), Institute for Architecture and Urban Studies, New York 1979.

Ghyka, Matila
Le nombre d'or, Paris 1931.

Ghyka, Matila
The Geometry of Art and Life, Dover Publications, New York 1946.

Giedion, Sigfried
Space, Time and Architecture, Harvard University Press, Cambridge 1941.

Gresleri, Giuliano and Zannier, Italo
Le Corbusier, Viaggio in Oriente, Venice 1984.

Hervé, Lucien
Le Corbusier as Artist, as Writer, Editions du Griffon, Neuchâtel 1970.

Hilpert, Thilo
Le Corbusier, Atelier der Ideen, Genius/ Christians und Reim Verlag, Hamburg 1987.

Huse, Norbert
Le Corbusier, Rowohlt Verlag, Hamburg 1976.

Le Corbusier
Vers une architecture, Paris 1922; English edition: *Towards a New Architecture*, translated by Frederick Etchells, London 1927/48.

Le Corbusier
Urbanisme, Paris 1925; English edition: *The City of Tomorrow and Its Planning*, translated by Frederick Etchells, London 1947.

Le Corbusier
Le Voyage d'Orient, Editions Forces Vives, Paris 1966.

Le Corbusier
L' avion accuse ..., *Aircraft*, The Studio Ltd., London 1935, and Fondation Le Corbusier, Paris and Editrice Abitare Segeste, Milan 1996.

Le Corbusier
Essential Le Corbusier, L'Esprit Nouveau Articles, reprint of articles from *L'Esprit Nouveau* by Le Corbusier dating from 1923–27, Architectural Press, Oxford 1998.

Le Corbusier
Le Modulor, Editions de l'architecture, Paris 1950; English edition: *The Modulor*, translated by Peter de Franca and Anna Bostock, London 1954.

Le Corbusier
Modulor 2, Editions de l'architecture, Paris 1955; English edition: *Modulor 2*, translated by Peter de Franca and Anna Bostock, London 1958.

Michels, Karen
Der Sinn der Unordnung, Arbeitsformen im Atelier Le Corbusier, Vieweg Verlag, Braunschweig/Wiesbaden 1989.

Palazzolo, Carlo and Vio, Riccardo (ed.)
In the Footsteps of Le Corbusier, with essays by various authors, Rizzoli International Publications, New York 1991.

Riehl, Martin
Vers une architecture: Das moderne Bauprogramm des Le Corbusier, Scaneg-Verlag, Munich 1992.

Roth, Alfred
Zwei Wohnhäuser von Le Corbusier und Pierre Jeanneret, Akad. Verlag Dr. Wedekind, Stuttgart 1928 and Karl Krämer Verlag, Stuttgart 1977.

Rowe, Colin and Slutzky, Robert
Transparency, Perspecta 8, The Yale Architectural Journal, New Haven 1964; new edition with a commentary by Bernhard Hoesli and an introduction by Werner Oechslin, Birkhäuser – Publishers for Architecture, Basel, Boston, Berlin 1997.

Rowe, Colin
The Mathematics of the Ideal Villa and Other Essays, The MIT Press, Cambridge 1976.

Russell, Frank (ed.)
Le Corbusier, Early Works by Charles-Edouard Jeanneret-Gris, Architectural Monographs, with essays by Geoffrey Baker and Jaques Gubler, Academy Editions, London and New York 1987.

Sekler, Mary/Patricia May
The Early Drawings of Charles-Edouard Jeanneret (Le Corbusier) 1902–1908, diss. Harvard University, Cambridge 1973, New York 1977.

Serenyi, Peter
Timeless but of its Time: Le Corbusier's Architecture in India, in: Perspecta 20, The Yale Architectural Journal, Yale University, New Haven and The MIT Press, Cambridge 1983.

Taylor, Brian Brace
Le Corbusier et Pessac, 1914–1928, 2 vols, Fondation Le Corbusier, Paris in co-operation with Harvard University, Cambridge, Paris 1972.

Turner, Paul Venable
The Education of Le Corbusier, A Study of the Development of Le Corbusier's Thought 1900–1920, diss. Harvard University, Cambridge 1971, New York 1977.

Vogt, Adolf Max
Le Corbusier, der edle Wilde. Zur Archäologie der Moderne, Vieweg Verlag, Braunschweig/Wiesbaden 1996.

Von Moos, Stanislaus
Le Corbusier, Elemente einer Synthese, Deutsche Verlags-Anstalt, Stuttgart 1968; English edition: *Le Corbusier. Elements of a Synthesis*, Cambridge, Mass. 1979.

Wedepohl, Edgar
Die Weissenhofsiedlung der Werkbundausstellung 'Die Wohnung' in Stuttgart, Wasmuths Monatshefte für Baukunst XI, Westermann Verlag, Braunschweig 1927.

Wittkower, Rudolf
Systems of Proportions, Architects' Yearbook 5, Journal of the Warburg and Courtauld Institutes, London 1953.

Wittkower, Rudolf
Architectural Principles in the Age of Humanism, London 1949 and London and New York 1952.

Zeising, Adolf,
Schriften zur Proportionslehre, Leipzig 1875.

Villa Savoye, 1929–1931 Poissy near Paris, living-room •

Le Corbusier

Paris ———— Chandigarh